BF
408
.G32
1996

CLEARI

Chicago Public Library

R0129046642

Creativity : how to catch lightning

CREATIVITY

How to Catch Lightning in a Bottle

George Gamez, Ph.D.

A Comprehensive Program for Unleashing Your Creative Power

P·E·A·K
Publications

Peak Publications
Los Angeles, Californi

D0167204

Creativity: How to Catch Lightning in a Bottle

Published by:

Peak Publications
Post Office Box 451067
P·E·A·K
Publications Los Angeles, CA 90045

All Rights Reserved. No part of this publication may be reproduced or transmitted, in any form or by any means, electronic or mechanical, including photocopying, recording or by any information storage and retrieval system without the prior written permission of the author, except for the inclusion of brief quotations in a review.

Copyright © 1996 by George Gamez
First printing 1996
Printed in the United States of America
1 2 3 4 5 6 7 8 9 10

Publisher's Cataloging in Publication
(Prepared by Quality Books Inc.)
Gamez, George.
    Creativity : how to catch lightning in a bottle / George Gamez.
    —1st ed.
    p. cm.
    Includes bibliographical references and index.
    LCCN: 96-67535.
    ISBN 0-9650590-3-0

    1. Creative ability.   I. Title.
    BF408.G36 1996   153'.35
                                QBI96-20230

Cover design and illustration by Lightbourne Images, copyright © 1996.

ACKNOWLEDGMENTS

Although many people have contributed to the making of this book, I accept full responsibility for any of its shortcomings. I wish I could acknowledge each of the contributors individually, but space permits listing only a few.

Most of all, I would like to thank my editor, Lizbeth Ferrant, for her invaluable and tireless support in all phases of the manuscript preparation. She did a thorough job of cleaning up my words and making countless recommendations along the way.

Thanks also to everyone who read various chapter drafts and made helpful suggestions. Among these were Gerald Alpert, M.S., Swami Beyondananda, Eleanor Fields, Ph.D., Richard Fobe, Allen Klein, Chuck Nagell, and Dean Simonton, Ph.D.

Last but not least, thanks to my family, friends and colleagues for their support and positive feedback, particularly in the selection of the book title.

CREDITS

I thank the following for permission to use copyrighted material:

For Gestalt figure in Chapter 1. Edwin G. Boring, "A new ambiguous figure," American Journal of Psychology. Copyright 1930, 1978 by the Board of Trustees of the University of Illinois Press. Used with permission of the University of Illinois Press.

For quote in Chapter 3, "The path to ones' own heaven . . . ," by Frederich Nictzsche, *Beyond Good and Evil,* translated by Walter Kaufmann and R. J. Hollingdale, Vintage Books, 1973.

For the "Removing an appendix . . . ." puzzle: Reprinted with permission of Sterling Publishing Co., Inc., 387 Park Ave. S., NY, NY 10016, from *Great Lateral Thinking Puzzles* by Paul Sloane & Des MacHale, © 1994 by Paul Sloane & Des MacHale.

For the "4th of July in England" puzzle: Reprinted with permission of Sterling Publishing C., Inc., 387 Park Ave. S., NY, NY 10016, from

Great Lateral Thinking Puzzles by Paul Sloane & Des MacHale, © 1994 by Paul Sloane & Des MacHale.

For "Another thing that I observed . . . ." Herbert Weinstock quoting Rossini in Rossini, 1968, by permission from Oxford University Press.

For Swami's jokes in Chapter 11, permission personally granted by the Swami himself.

For story about P. F. Sloane in Chapter 3 excerpted from "P. F. Sloan Returns" by Paul Zollo, from *Songtalk* the journal of the National Academy of Songwriters, Winter 1991.

For coed's letter to parents: Allen Klein, *The Healing Power of Humor*, 1989.

For "a new studio in the attic . . . ." excerpted from Pierre Daix, *Picasso, Life and Art*, used by permission of the publisher, Harper Collins Publishers 1993.

Copyediting by Sue Irwin

Book design and typography by Cirrus Design

Warning-Disclaimer

This book is designed to provide information to help the reader become more creative.

Every effort has been make to make this book as accurate and complete as possible. However, there is always room for error and mistakes.

The purpose of the book is to educate and entertain. The author and Peak Publications shall have neither liability nor responsibility to any person or entity with respect to any loss or damage caused or alleged to be caused, directly or indirectly, by the information contained in this book.

If you do not wish to be bound by the above, you may return this book to the publisher for a full refund.

CONTENTS

Foreword

BY JACK SEGAL

Many years after I achieved some success and stature in the songwriting field, I was invited to teach that subject at California State University, Northridge. I asked my students what they wanted to know. Of course, they wanted to acquire skills such as form, content, music, lyrics, melody, rhythm, harmony, rhyming, etc. They doted upon my intimacy with the famous and near-famous recording legends, writers, producers.

But surprisingly, they wanted to know more about the process of inspiration. The super-creative moment, from advent to completion, was a mystery to me. However, I could tell them about such sequences concerning "Scarlet Ribbons" and "When Sunny Gets Blue." Good stories but much remained unexplained. As I related these events, more about inspiration, creativity, and what to do in this arcane instance occurred to me. And still I failed to totally reveal to my students the "idea," the spate of initial lyrics and music. I invented the phrase, "catching lightning in a bottle," to instruct about handling the impact and getting the first furious ideas down without inhibiting the flow. The later, ultimate form through editing was easier to recall. But what was this "thing" all about?

There was a paucity of source material on the subject. I became frustrated about my inability to enlighten. Fellow writers were not forthcoming, either through disinterest or a lack of information. Sammy Cahn said, "First comes the phone call, then I go to work. What's inspiration got to do with it?" I asked Johnny Mercer, my mentor, why he wrote so many songs about birds—"Mr. Meadowlark," "Bob White," "Skylark," "Cuckoo In The Clock." Johnny smiled and said, "I guess I just love our fine-feathered friends." Bobby Troupe: "Don't know a thing about it. I just use it and I'm grateful for the gift."

What about excitement, physical signals, the gut-feeling that "something" was about to happen? No intelligible responses, more's the pity. The song "Something's Coming" from *West Side Story* tells tons about that strong, strange premonition!

I remember George Gamez in the Cal State class, and later, in the SGA (Songwriters Guild of America) seminars. As writer-guitarist-singer, he was wonderful. But when I raised the question of creativity, his eyes brightened and his body language indicated a fierce interest. While most of my information was emotional and subjective, I could have predicted that George would investigate the unfathomable in search of academic, objective answers and find the credible sources I never discovered.

Well, here is the Gamez book, and I find it admirable in every way. It contains *so much:* The environmental influences, nurturing over abuse, the fostering of talent and imagination, the sequence of intuitive breakthroughs, practical exercises in moral and spiritual behavior and creativity enhancement, myths and truths, collaboration, stimulating brain activity, the role of dreams, inspiration and perspiration, the later editing process, the "zone," the "pocket," and the "groove."

George Gamez investigates the positive and negative forces that develop or kill the inherent potentials of all artists. In all this scope and depth, he ignores the caveat, "Fools rush in where angels fear to tread." Clarification on all essences of the subject has rarely yielded so much of the prize. Thank you, George, for being a damned fool!

Fools pursue insight at all costs. The mountain climber scales Everest because it is *there!*

One last observation suggested by this book. The greatest scientists of all ages have maintained that they recognized the "presence" of some higher power when they seemed able to do something much better than they *knew how* to do. They only succeeded when they turned to "reading the mind of God!" What a concept! At last, a spiritual key to the enigmas that persist. God goads the climber to the crest of the mountain, and when the desired destination is reached, *God is there!* And most certainly, He is *in* the process of Inspired Creativity, that which happens in a split second and is accompanied by instant insight and the spiritual will to get it all *down!* To grab "lightning in a bottle," to express it , to try to perfect it—on paper, the music staff, the clay, the canvas, the stage—welcomes the presence of the "Mind of God!" I truly believe George Gamez was always searching for Him, and I know he succeeded!

INTRODUCTION

It has taken me a lifetime to get here. This book is a culmination of my experience in three different creative professions: psychology, music/songwriting, and business. I'm delighted you're joining me in this exciting quest to develop your creativity. Designed for people who want more out of life, this book is about getting and using creative power and passion everyday.

I received my first important lessons about the psychology of the creative process through the humanistic psychology movement, which arose as a reaction against both behaviorism and Freud's teachings. Behaviorism argues that it is behavior that counts, and that what goes on inside a person is not important. Freud, on the other hand, reduced man to a bundle of basic drives, such as sex. The humanistic psychology movement began calling itself the Third Force—teaching that what goes on inside the individual is important and that behavior is motivated not just by basic drives, but by higher goals.

I began flirting with the forces underlying creativity when I started attending humanistic psychology conventions and workshops in the 1960s and '70s. It was an inspiring time—the whole personal growth movement was opening up wide!

Gestalt, existential and Jungian psychologies, as well as Eastern philosophy, were expanding our collective consciousness and nurturing our spiritual growth. Gestalt and existential psychology emphasized freedom and choice, bringing back individual responsibility. Eastern philosophy and Jungian psychology helped us see that the individual psyche can only be fully understood when placed in the context of a larger consciousness. It was a time of real breakthrough. We were no longer restricted to thinking about ourselves in the confining, limited terms painted by behaviorism and Freudian reductionism.

Today I still cherish those years. It was a time of great inter- and intrapersonal growth. Each day was an adventure and an opening up to new possibilities and inquiries. During that time I began to realize that there is an intimate relationship between psychology and the arts. Both domains deal with feelings and intuition—searching the inner world to create a better outer world.

Humanistic psychology encouraged me to integrate my interests in psychology with my passion for music. As a result, I financed my college education by playing flamenco guitar in coffeehouses and college concerts, and I even recorded an album entitled *A Modern Touch of Latin.*

Music is still an integral part of my life. Its joys and its disappointments have been a wonderful source for discovering specific techniques to enhance the creative process. Over the years, I have written many songs and joined songwriting workshops. Through these workshops, with such great talents as Arthur Hamilton ("Cry Me a River") and Al Kasha *(If They Ask You, You Can Write a Song)*, I learned how songwriters deal with their creative blocks and how they polish vinyl (or plastic or metal) into gold by writing, rewriting and digging into the deeper resources of the creative mind. Working with first-rate musicians in the recording studio, I succeeded in having one of my songs recorded by the world-class talent, Jose Feliciano.

Around 1981, Jack Segal (writer of "When Sunny Gets Blue") became my songwriting mentor. Jack lives a truly artistic life and is able to dramatically describe the creative process and provide inspiration to his students. He is a great story teller and has some great accounts about "catching lightning in a bottle."

In 1984 I entered a third domain when I established a mental health clinic. This was a world I previously believed to be totally devoid of creativity. Was I wrong!

Even though I had formerly served as director of a mental health clinic for the County of Los Angeles, I was sick with worry about going out on my own. I feared failure, and my own inner critic reminded me constantly of the dangers involved in my proposed venture. Working through the fear by reviewing my own writings about the power of creative risk-taking, I listened to my inner mentor and plunged in.

During the next ten years, I learned more about the relationship between creativity and business than I had ever imagined possible. My psychology clinic grew beyond my most optimistic dreams. I hired psychologists, psychiatrists and other mental health professionals, along with a support staff. Then I had to learn how to run a corporation. Working on the principles that openness and flexibility are pre-requisites to creativity, and that creative solutions are essential in good management and administration, I taught myself management techniques and oversaw the work of 26 employees. Of course there were crises aplenty. But I knew I had to persevere. I used creative principles to spruce up my marketing, and by doing so, ran a highly successful clinic.

One of the jobs I hated most was negotiating settlements with insurance companies. It drove me crazy the way they used endless ploys to avoid paying their bills. Still I had to admire them for their constant creativity in putting me off. "Our computers are down," "Mr. Johnson, the adjuster, no longer works on that file," "Please send me that information again," "She's in a meeting." Their litany was long, the results the same. Payment delayed, or payment denied.

So I went them one better, with creative techniques to force them to pay. For example, I learned about my legal rights and began filing in court. I also learned that silence is a powerful and creative negotiating technique. At the right places in a negotiation, it can force the other party to come forth and respond to your offers.

As time went on, I developed creativity workshops with screen writers, songwriters and actors. I literally worked with thousands of clients, helping them overcome creative blocks. What you're about to read is the result of those years spent in one-on-one and group cre-ativity sessions.

One of psychology's common themes is that we live in a repressed society where most people live lives of quiet desperation. Quite simply, the source of so much unhappiness and dissatisfaction lies in being trapped in rigid patterns of conformity.

I believe we have a choice. What's better, living in strict obedience to traditions, authority and institutions—in effect never seeing the sunlight—or finding a way to break through to experience the real rush of creativity?

You already know the answer, or you would not have read this far. Of course, no world is as black or white as I have painted it. Nevertheless, even if you feel mildly restless and need to find "something" you love, there's a world of pleasure in unleashing your creative forces.

You may not know exactly where you're heading, but I promise you'll be all the richer and happier for it once you get moving!

THE STRUCTURE OF THE BOOK

I have structured this book to follow the stages of the hero's journey. Joseph Campbell, in analyzing the hero mythologies of many cultures, has demonstrated that the hero's adventure in these stories follows a pattern. The hero's journey generally involves a call to adventure, the adventure itself and a return home. The journey into developing your creativity is an adventure which follows the same pattern.

The first section begins where every hero's journey begins: with a call to adventure. To help you answer the call, we will clear the way by separating fact from fiction.

In the second section, we begin the adventure and become explorers. We are seekers of wisdom, in search of answers. We look at stages of the creative process, the personality traits of creative persons, and the environmental requirements for increasing creativity.

For those souls who persevere and endure, the third section continues the adventure and will reward them with untold treasures. We will dig in and acquire new tools of the quest. These are more specific methods and techniques for further enhancing creativity. They include self-hypnosis, affirmations, Neuro Linguistic Programming, visualization, language systems and a variety of problem-solving techniques.

Finally, we reach the summit, conquer our demons and become transformed in the process of completing our journey. As we return home, we give birth to a more powerful and confident creator within. We will have gained new insights into the creative process and what it takes to go on to greater challenges. Our journey through this book will prepare us for the next level of creative development. The end of one journey is the beginning of the next.

PART ONE

A CALL TO ADVENTURE: THE CHALLENGE

You must do the thing you think you cannot do.

Eleanor Roosevelt

CHAPTER I

CREATIVITY: WHO'S GOT IT?

In the beginning God created the Heaven and the Earth: and the Earth was without form and void and darkness was upon the face of the deep.

Genesis 1:1-2

The deeper one looks, the more our valuations disappear— meaninglessness approaches! We have created the world that possesses values! Knowing this, we know too, that reverence for truth is already the consequence of an illusion—and that one should value more than truth the force that forms, simplifies, shapes, invents.

Frederich Nietzsche

"WHAT, ME CREATIVE?"

Yes, you. I firmly believe that we are *all* creative *all* the time. By the time you finish this chapter, I think you'll agree. My goal is to make you feel more creative, to show that you *are* creative on a day-to-day basis, and to give you workable new skills and techniques that will constantly reinforce this concept. Believing that you are creative will help you become more creative every day.

You are probably interested in creativity, or you wouldn't be reading this book. Perhaps you've daydreamed about producing something novel but don't have a clue how to begin. Or maybe, as a professional, you want to get a competitive edge on your rivals. Maybe you want to be more innovative as a lawyer, writer, musician, visual artist or inventor. On the other hand, maybe you feel you've *never* been creative. Whatever the case, you've come to the right place.

Are you raising children or managing a family? Are you nurturing someone's creativity by being a parent, sponsor, mentor, teacher or therapist? Understanding higher creativity is a great way to enhance your relationships *and* your own personal growth.

WEBSTER'S DEFINITION

What is creativity? What does it mean to be creative? *Webster's New World Dictionary* defines creativity as "the ability to create" and create is defined as "To cause, to come into existence, to bring into being, to give rise to, to portray for the first time."

Being creative, then, means to engage in some activity that causes something new to come into existence or into being. It seems like a simple definition, but if you look at it more closely, it isn't. It just brings up more questions like: What is existence? What is being?

THE NATURE OF REALITY

Psychologists and physicists say the world is forever changing and we never encounter the same world twice. Look around you. Outside, autos race by, sounds of construction permeate the air and the weather and seasons are changing. At home, you're working on the lawn, buying new furniture or rearranging a room—all to please your sense of "ideal" reality.

Everything moves, albeit imperceptibly at times. Even a supposedly solid object like a chair is changing. At the very least, its color is fading. At a deeper level, the molecules making up the chair are in flux. In fact, scientists say that any solid object is really a field of energy in constant motion.

We are, ourselves, a bundle of creative energy. Some of us just don't know it yet!

WE ARE *ALL* CREATIVE

Every day, we express creativity in the way we dress, our lifestyles, the way we speak, what we cook and in virtually every decision we make. From dieting to dating, financing a home to building a house, or selling a car, there's creativity inherent in all our activities.

In fact, you just can't escape being creative! With the universe in such a constant state of flux, we're all in a constant state of transformation.

CREATIVITY IS ORGANIZATION

Reality is an energy field with a vast array of shapes, sizes, colors, textures and smells. These can be grouped in various ways to form objects. How each of us organizes these shapes, colors and textures is an innate act of creativity.

For example, take the following series of dots:

    ...   .

How would you group these dots? Would you view the subgroups with three, four and five dots as a group, and say that there are two such groups side by side? If so, your organization would look like this:

    ...   .

Maybe you'd group them with the four inner subgroups constituting a single entity. If so, they would look like this:

    ...   .

As you see, this grouping would yield a total of three objects: two objects made of three dots at each end and an object in the middle made of four subgroups.

What this shows is that the way that the world is divided into objects is somewhat arbitrary. Aristotle divided nature into plants, minerals and animals. He could have divided the world in other ways. The manner in which he chose to organize the world was really not an act of discovery; it was an act of creative invention.

How we organize the world around us is also an act of creativity. For example, we are being creative when we group and organize furniture.

Think about your house or apartment. Where did you put the sofa? Is it next to the television set? Did you group the coffee table next to the sofa, or in front of the sofa, or beside the sofa? Whatever your design, your manner of organizing the furniture was creative.

IS SEEING REALLY BELIEVING?

Look at Figure 1. You can take the same "reality" and organize it in more than one way to see two different figures. Depending on how you group the lines, you'll see either a young woman or an old lady. Same lines, but two totally different realities. Look—the jaw of the young woman can also be the nose of the old lady. The mouth of the old lady is the young woman's necklace, and the old lady's right eye is the young woman's earlobe. If you still have trouble seeing

Figure 1.

both figures, try seeing the young woman's neckline as the old lady's chin. It's visual proof that organizing *is* creating.

Did you know that Eskimos can differentiate between hundreds of different types of snow? Or that desert dwellers can differentiate many different stages in the pregnancy of a camel? It's quite arbitrary whether we group items as two, or three, four or an infinite number of events or objects. It just depends upon the needs of the observer.

IMAGINING IS CREATING

Imagination is the key to creativity. Einstein is credited with saying, "Imagination is more important than knowledge."

What *is* imagination? It's another whole universe of objects just waiting to be organized. Only this time, the objects are internal rather than external.

We make replicas of external objects in our minds and then manipulate and experiment with them. Some psychologists call this "vicarious trial and error." The objects of the imagination are obviously not real. By manipulating them, it's easy to learn more about the world. It's a lot safer too—you don't have to jump from a 20-foot ladder to know that you're risking a broken leg at the very least. You don't have to paint the kitchen to view it as red with green flowers (a nightmare if ever I visualized one!)

Through creativity, you can make the leap from envisioning to reality. Your own imagination is the key to an abundant and fruitful creative life.

MANY AREAS OF CREATIVITY

There are all kinds of ways to exercise your creativity—from cooking to dieting to dating. The salesman who wants to outsell his competitors must be creative in his bidding and use his imagination to win the order—and possibly an incentive prize from his employer. Builder, architect and entrepreneur all engage daily in the process of creativity.

On the domestic scene, home buyers and their brokers exercise their creativity by finding new ways to finance a mortgage. For example, the seller can hold the second mortgage, or the house can be financed with an adjustable rate mortgage instead of a fixed rate. The down payment can come from a partner, a parent or a rich uncle. The term, *creative financing* has found a permanent home in our language over the last several years.

We express creativity every day, from the moment we wake up until the moment we fall asleep. Some psychologists say that even dreams are a reflection of creativity at work.

If we're all so creative, what's the problem? It's figuring out how to channel and focus creativity into specific areas that are meaningful to you. For example, you may be very creative as an engineer and want to cross over into songwriting. You may be an innovative baker, yet long to hang up your apron and start cooking with words in the arena of advertising. Mid-life career changers are especially caught between desiring new lives and feeling that they've worked too hard and long at the old one to make a meaningful fresh start.

WHY CREATIVITY HAS GOTTEN A BAD RAP

In primitive times, creativity centered around the basic struggle for life. Humans spent most of their time in search of food, clothing and shelter. Pottery making, weaving cloth, and the production of weapons and tools were all done by ordinary individuals in the community. The technical skills required to produce something new and important for the community were not complex. Creativity itself may or may not have been highly valued. It was probably not seen as anything separate from daily living.

As society evolved and became more complex, people specialized. Eventually, individuals who were highly skilled in one area formed groups around trades, crafts and professions. A high level of skill became a requirement for entry into these groups, and everyday creativity became less valued.

What an individual created would then be compared to similar products created by others equally or more highly trained. Creativity began to be judged by peer review, rather than by the community at large.

Our modern world has evolved to where we've become obsessed with what others think. Spiritual values have decreased in importance. We live in an era of fierce competition, and we measure our activities by how well they lead us toward materialistic goals. That's not a judgment call. It's simply a fact.

We no longer value activity solely for the purpose of recreation, creating a sense of community or enhancing spiritual values. In short, we measure our worth by "success," whatever that means to each of us.

In this competitive, success-driven society our creations are valued by the potential they have for bringing us the primary "desirables"—money, sex and power. There's increased pressure to create products that meet the narrow criteria of the marketplace or help us survive in this complex, "gotta-win-the-prize" arena. Working in a highly competitive environment, you're constantly under pressure to produce products (or services, tangible or intangible) that stand up to the competition.

With this new demand for focused and often complex creativity in a marketplace filled with highly skilled and competitive rivals, creativity becomes "a problem." It becomes even more valued and specialized, being measured against a yardstick of getting ahead in the material world. It is not enough for you to be creative; your product must be original, innovative and marketable in today's society. With the pressure on, you may "choke."

WHY BEING CREATIVE IS NOT ENOUGH

While we all make a host of creative decisions daily in the course of our lives, these don't necessarily yield "The Big Payoff." Your questions about creativity become more specific: "How can I become more original or prolific in my creativity? How can I channel my creativity into one very special field? How can I get an edge on the competition?"

HOW DO I BEGIN?

1. **First off, relax . . . and realize that originality doesn't come in one big bang.**

   Years ago, I discovered that the bulk of true originality comes from constantly modifying your work, rather than from creating in one flash of genius. Let me show you what I mean.

   Paco de Lucia. Paco is a flamenco and jazz guitarist par excellence—an innovator of great originality. Beginning as a child prodigy in Spain, he had already revolutionized Flamenco guitar playing by the age of 13.

   When I met Paco in Algeciras, Spain, he was very athletic and used to take a daily swim in the Mediterranean. He would swim in an arc halfway across to Gibraltar and back. From my nearby hotel room, I saw people standing on the beach, watching this human fish swimming way far out in the distance. Later, he would come back and we'd drink coffee and play the guitar.

   Paco continued to modify traditional flamenco by infusing it with modern harmonies. Besides pushing the limits of traditional rhythms, he experimented with new chords.

   In turn, I had learned to play Bossa Nova songs composed of modern chordal harmonies. As I played these pieces, Paco watched me intently. Sometimes he'd ask me to play a particular piece again. The next day I'd be delightfully surprised when I heard him incorporate this or that Bossa Nova chord into his playing. That's right—the genius was learning from me!

   Paco took small musical bits or new chords and incorporated them into his own flamenco style. He was constantly modifying his playing on a day-to-day, minute-to-minute basis, always making variations. If you heard him at two different times, months or years apart, you would think, "My God, what originality." You wouldn't know all of the little modifications and work that went into his changes, day by day and week by week.

   Often, we try too hard to be original and wind up highly frustrated because of the mistaken notion that true originality springs forth full blown. Even Einstein said that the reason he was able to create and formulate his new theories was because he stood on the shoulders of giants. One of those giants was Sir Isaac Newton who, when asked how he was able to discover the law of universal gravitation, answered, "By thinking on it continuously."

So get a leg up. Stand on the shoulders of someone you admire. Learn from them, and use the originality that comes in small bursts, based on your existing knowledge. Modify what you have. Play around with the material at hand and continuously think about it. Over the long haul, you'll be able to create an impressive body of work.

2. Remember that creativity is basic problem-solving.

Here's another anecdote that illustrates an important, but overlooked creative key.

Years ago, I was driving a disaster-riddled, ten-year-old clunker. One hot summer day, it developed a water leak. I took it to a gas station where the mechanic opened the hood and determined that my water heater hose had sprung a leak.

"I'll have to take the fender off to get to the hose," he said. "That'll be $60.00."

Besides being nearly broke, in my gut I felt this was a rip-off. I took the car down the street for a second opinion. At this second gas station, the attendant, who was not a mechanic, hit upon a simple, creative solution. He cut the hose in two, removed the piece where the hole was, placed a metal tube in each end of the cut hose, pushed the two sides flush with each other and clamped the whole thing tightly shut. No need to remove the fender. Total cost: $2.00 for parts and labor!

I was thrilled to have saved all that money and amazed by this perfect example of everyday creativity. Instead of taking a conventional approach, the attendant solved the problem in a new and innovative way. He wasn't an expert mechanic, but in this case he didn't have to be. (Perhaps if he'd "known better," he wouldn't have been so willing to try something radical.)

The moral is: Don't get stuck on one solution to a problem. If you want to get something done and the old ways don't work, there's bound to be a simpler, and, possibly, more efficient solution. You just have to be flexible and use your imagination.

CREATIVITY EXERCISE PROGRAM

Exercise your muscles regularly and you see results. Same with creativity. Some creativity guides insist that you do a writing exercise every day. Not me. I do believe, however, that it's important to exercise your creative imagination. The more you do it, the more you'll want to do it.

I prefer more individual guidelines. Go ahead and develop your own routine. Do some of the tasks that you're interested in daily. If you're a writer, write. If you're a musician, play. If you're a painter, paint. If you're an athlete or dancer, do some physical exercise. When you get tired of your routine, change it. Throughout this book you'll get ideas to enhance your creativity and incorporate them into your daily program.

That's it. My daily creativity exercise regimen. You don't even have to do it daily, but at least make the effort three times a week, for at least one hour at a time. Like most exercise, three one-hour sessions are better than one three-hour marathon.

If you're passionately involved in some creative project, forget about the exercise. Go ahead and pursue your passion. Whatever you do, the more you do it, the more creative you'll become.

CHAPTER 2

CREATIVITY: FACT AND FICTION

*. . . I will argue instead that making sense of the development
of creative works requires no elaborate construction, because
creativity is firmly rooted in past experience and has its source
in the same thought processes that we all use every day.*

Robert W. Weisberg, *Creativity:*
Beyond the Myth of Genius

For years I lived in awe of geniuses. Most people do. I read about
and admired great historical figures such as Newton, Einstein
and Mozart. Contemporary men and women of high achievement
such as Carl Jung (psychoanalyst), Simone de Beauvoir (feminist
writer), Ben Franklin (inventor/statesman) and the Beatles (pop
musicians) were also high on my list. Their extraordinary achieve-
ments truly amazed me and I saw them as a breed separate and
special.

I also believed that these geniuses created their works by inspiration, and that their special gifts were just bestowed upon them by
some magical waving of God's wand. Sound familiar?

My research and clinical experience, however, showed this:
These "geniuses" were "made, not born." They may have had some
special gifts at birth. More importantly, however, they, or significant

others, nurtured and developed these talents from an early age. We now know that much hard work and perspiration went into the careers of these creators. Besides gaining skills and knowledge in a particular field or domain, they had models and teachers who encouraged them to analyze and modify. Parents and mentors encouraged them to experiment and explore new ways of dealing with what they had already learned.

At some point in their lives, each of these individuals discovered the most important key to creativity. *They actively used their imaginations to go beyond their knowledge.*

WHAT WE DIDN'T LEARN IN SCHOOL

Remember school? What did we learn there? If your experience was anything like mine, you learned to memorize and regurgitate information and mimic the teacher or professor. The better we did this, the better we succeeded.

Unfortunately, this process made us passive learners, absorbing knowledge like the proverbial sponge. I'm sure you were frequently told that "knowledge is power" and that "college graduates make more money over their lifetimes than those who drop out of school early."

What most of us didn't learn was how to take the knowledge presented at school and go beyond it. We didn't learn to use our creative imaginations.

Worse than not learning anything about the creative process, we repeatedly heard a commonly held misconception: "creativity cannot be taught." I'm sure you also heard that highly creative people are "born and not made." Little wonder then, that in all my 20 years of formal education, I never took a course in creativity enhancement. The schools I went to never offered any!

In learning music from my guitar teacher, Eduardo Freeman, I encountered the same orientation. I will be forever grateful to him for teaching me to play the guitar. He taught me the works of the great masters, which I learned to perform masterfully. However, I regret to say that he never directed me to take an existing melody or chord progression and modify it or change it, even in the smallest way. What existed was sacred and I dared not tamper with it in any way.

In addition, I thought that musical compositions popped up full blown. By an inspirational process, a composition would magically and beautifully spring forth just as easily as a rose opens in spring. If only half-baked ideas came into my mind, I became discouraged that I didn't have the gift. I was waiting passively for full blown ideas rather than actively improving on the germinal musical ideas flashing into my consciousness. I let my brain idle and rejected *mental and cognitive processes.* These were not supposed to be involved in real creativity . . . at least not in the field of music.

Years later, I studied at the Dick Grove School of Music in Los Angeles and took classes in improvisation, composition and arranging. I had an opportunity to flex my creativity muscles and began composing my own music and songs. Fortunately, I found good teachers who challenged my creative imagination. I learned to actively transform small flashes of insight into large bolts of lightning.

Still, I am left with gnawing questions: What is happening to the thousands, if not millions of people who are taught these myths and misconceptions? How is the creativity of children being stifled at the local neighborhood music store or high school class? What about the young people aspiring to make their mark in business, the sciences and in the various trades? How many creative minds are wasted through neglect or wrong teachings?

THE TOP TEN

One of my reasons for writing this book is to discuss and dispel deadly notions about creativity. Below are what I believe to be the ten worst myths and misconceptions about the creative process.

MYTH #1. To Be Creative, You Must Be Totally Original

Originality is not synonymous with creativity. In fact, you can measure your creativity by various criteria besides originality. J. P. Guilford, noted creativity researcher and past president of the

American Psychological Association, developed tests to measure originality, flexibility, fluency and elaborateness.

■ Originality

Originality is measured by how *unusual* your product is, or how much it differs from the norm. You will be considered original if you create unusual products. Before Dumbo, a flying elephant was an original idea. Today, a mousetrap is no longer original, unless it is very unusual. Although originality may be an important characteristic of geniuses such as Picasso or Einstein, it is but one aspect of creativity.

■ Fluency

The second criterion for evaluating creativity is fluency. Guilford defines fluency simply as the *quantity* of creative products produced, without regard for originality. Thus, a craftsperson making hundreds of coffee mugs, all of which are very similar, would be labeled creative, although not very original.

■ Flexibility

Flexibility, on the other hand, measures *how many different* (not necessarily unusual) products you can create. A flexible architect can design houses with many different configurations. He can build homes that are functional in summer climates or more suitable for colder environments. Some may have two stories and others three. They may all be traditional Spanish style houses but different from each other in the attributes just mentioned. Although he may not be creating unusual or extremely novel products, we still consider him creative.

■ Elaboration

The ability to elaborate is the fourth aspect of creativity and it refers to how much *detail and specificity* you include in your work. We all differ in our capacity to produce intricate and complex works. Again, you are creative when you produce extremely complex and detailed designs even if they are neither unusual nor large in number.

So there you are. You can be highly creative without being in the least bit original. You can be fluent (prolific) or flexible (produce many different but not unusual products). Likewise, you might invent elaborate (complex) but conventional and unoriginal designs and still be labeled creative.

MYTH #2. Only Artists and Scientists Are Creative.

Most people have this misconception, consciously or unconsciously, and pay a high price for it. This idea can cause you to give up exercising your creativity muscles merely because you are not an artist or a scientist.

Throughout this book, you will see many examples of creativity that have nothing to do with art or science. Little Monica may be very creative in persuading her parents to buy her a new toy. I'm sure Bill Clinton would agree that developing a powerful campaign strategy is a very creative enterprise. Unfortunately, even murder and thievery can be creative.

According to the fourfold criteria developed by Guilford, non-artistic people can be more creative than many artists or scientists. A businessperson or inventor who generates many products is creative. A public relations person, a "top 500" CEO or a military general can find countless opportunities for creativity in their work.

On the other hand, an artist who produces one painting a year is not very fluent. He may even be extremely inflexible and unoriginal. Some artists create aesthetically pleasing works but merely imitate and copy. We've all listened to musicians play exact versions of what the top artists of the day are recording and most would agree that this art has limited creativity.

Abraham Maslow, psychologist and leader of the Human Potential Movement, once said "a first rate soup is more creative than a second rate painting."

MYTH #3. You Need a High IQ to Be Creative.

*I am not a genius. I'm not even gifted. I'm just your
garden-variety smart person.*

> **Peter Norton of Norton Disk
> Doctor, Norton Utilities,**
> *Los Angeles Times,* June 12, 1994

Most research shows that a high IQ is not required for creativity and may be negatively correlated with creativity. In other words, high intelligence may interfere with creativity in some areas.

The importance of IQ to creativity depends on the particular field of activity. In abstract fields such as mathematics, physics and astronomy, an IQ of at least 120 is probably necessary to be truly creative. However, in most fields, a high degree of intelligence would not be necessary. I doubt that IQ is that important in creative gardening or cooking.

According to Dean Simonton, author of *Genius, Creativity and Leadership,* "There just isn't any correlation between creativity and IQ. The average college graduate has an IQ of about 120, and that is enough to write novels, do scientific research, or any other kind of creative work."

In addition, some researchers are moving away from the simplistic notion of intelligence as measured by IQ tests. Howard Gardner, an eminent creativity researcher, has developed a theory of "multiple intelligences" that has been steadily gaining in popularity. He distinguishes between linguistic, musical, logical-mathematical, kinesthetic, spatial, interpersonal and intrapersonal intelligences.

Intelligence is manifested not only in abstract reasoning skills but in less intellectual areas as well. One of my clients, Dominica, is high in *interpersonal intelligence* because she is particularly adept in dealing with people. She is sensitive to their needs and is charming and likeable. She is a great saleswoman and public relations expert because she can think on her feet and create just the right campaign for her clients.

Elizabeth is particularly endowed with *spatial intelligence*. Because of this, she is a good painter and an expert at organizing office space and designing interiors.

Spatial intelligence is also important in musical ability, and some experts now define *musical intelligence* as an unusual sensitivity to space and sound.

The names of many successful dancers and athletes come to mind when we speak of kinesthetic intelligence. Isadora Duncan and Jim Thorpe had a sixth sense in using their bodies to define new realities. An excellent example of creativity using *kinesthetic intelligence* is an Oregon boy named Fosbury who invented the Fosbury flop, a method of high jumping over the bar backwards and head first. His invention won him an Olympic gold medal.

Having a way with words is a defining characteristic of *linguistic intelligence* and a skill needed by anyone aspiring to be a writer.

> *The reason for your complaint lies, it seems to me, in the constraint which your intellect imposes upon your imagination . . .it hinders the creative work of the mind—if the intellect examines too closely the ideas pouring in. . . .*
> **Friedrich Schiller**

MYTH #4. Creativity Means Producing Something Tangible.

This is only partially true. There are, in fact, many intangible ways in which you can be creative. In *The Creative Edge*, William Miller lists seven ways in which you can experience your creativity. Material creativity, where you make something concrete and tangible is only one of them. Here are six more:

▧ *Idea Creativity*

This includes an idea for a new game, a new way of cooking spaghetti, or a new way to market underwear. During brainstorming sessions, many ideas are created that are never used. These ideas, however, may give rise to other ideas. Contrary to some notions that ideas are cheap, generating new ideas is definitely an important creative act. Most of our modern inventions began with an idea.

▨ *Relationship Creativity*

Keeping relationships running smoothly and harmoniously requires imagination. Couples need inspiration and work to keep their relationships alive and interesting. Parents must creatively negotiate and reach compromises between feuding siblings.

▨ *Spontaneous Creativity*

When was the last time you told a joke at a party or sang a song with a karaoke machine? Spontaneous creativity is manifested in the improvisations of comedians and in the persuasive techniques of good salespeople. You can see it in the split-second decisions and improvisational changes of athletes like Michael Jordan, Martina Navratilova, Magic Johnson, Joe Montana and Jose Canseco. They experience a feeling of freedom in moments of spontaneous inspiration. Athletes call this feeling "the zone." Musicians call it "the groove" or "the pocket."

▨ *Event Creativity*

In 1991, I produced the 1st Annual Latin Music Expo, a day of workshops and panel discussions on the Latin music industry. In the evening, we showcased new Latin artists and had an awards ceremony. Jose Feliciano was presented with a lifetime achievement award.

I came to realize just how much hard work, planning and creativity go into producing such events. Tremendous amounts of effort and improvisation go into obtaining a suitable site for such an event, negotiating prices and persuading panelists and exhibitors to participate. We constantly brainstormed and problem-solved to sell and market the event.

Ask anyone who has ever planned a wedding or a party and they'll tell you how creative they had to be to make everything come out "just right."

▓ Organizational Creativity

Know anyone who seems to have a real knack for organizing? They are not only good at it, but they actually seem to enjoy it. Right? Organizations vary from the family unit to the neighborhood watch group to the National Democratic or Republican Conventions, and organizational creativity varies along these same dimensions. I especially admire individuals who organize rallies and support groups or build institutions to support worthy causes.

In our crime-ravaged cities, we are in great need of leaders with skills in community organizing. An article in the *Los Angeles Times* entitled "The New Neighborhood: Creating Connections Out of Chaos" reports how various community groups are working together to form new bonds of connectedness to improve their neighborhoods.

▓ Inner creativity

The ability to control and organize our inner world is also an act of creativity. Creating an inner world of peace and tranquility is a valuable skill. It can certainly help us manage our stress and keep our minds clear. Navigating the inner world of dreams and harmonizing conflicting elements of the inner world are other aspects of this type of creativity.

MYTH #5. Originality Is Inborn.

"You either have it or you don't." Sound familiar? But wait! We now know that originality comes from a process of constant analysis and repeated modification. We know that originality is learned. You start with imitation and, little by little, modify your work. The end product appears original only if we ignore all the stages of modification that went before it.

Anthony Blunt, in *Picasso's "Guernica"* (1969), writes that Picasso changed his style frequently and rapidly. He says that it was difficult to realize that the works of different periods were by the same artist. Works from the first period would be radically and fundamentally different from those of the second period. However, by following the steps and stages between the first paintings and the last, a discerning person could see that the changes had occurred by a sequence of "steps, each of which is intelligible and can be seen as following logically on the earlier moves, and each of which was arrived at by a process of experiment and thought."

Are there inborn and genetic differences between people? Definitely. One person can be innately more sensitive or flexible than another. However, psychological research shows that most of our rigidities and inflexibilities are learned. We develop and even create our personality structure through a process of socialization. Starting in childhood and throughout our lives, we are socialized to conform and learn to fear exploring and experimenting.

Sure, there are also genetic differences in temperament and physical abilities. These may be useful in drawing, playing the piano or hitting a home run. Nevertheless, whatever traits we are born with, throughout our lifetimes we continue molding and changing these inborn temperaments.

By changing rigid habits and improving your self image, you *can* teach yourself to be more original and flexible. In subsequent chapters, we explore how flexibility and your capacity for originality can be increased, modified, molded and expanded.

At this point, I must reiterate that originality is *only one aspect* of creativity. You can measure your creative abilities not only by how original your product or idea is, but also by the number and variety of these you generate.

MYTH #6. Creativity Is Easy.

> *It is not the critic who counts; not the man who points out how the strong man stumbled, or where the doer of deeds could have done them better. The credit belongs to the man who is actually in the arena.*
> **Theodore Roosevelt**

As the saying goes, "Creativity is 1 percent inspiration and 99 percent perspiration." Much hard work goes into most worthwhile projects. It is not easy and it is not all fun and games. Why? Because creativity involves struggling with all the demons and obstacles that keep you from fulfilling your greatest and your smallest dreams. It means picking yourself back up even when you have little strength left and the light of hope seems to be fading in the distance.

Creativity may be more or less difficult depending on the stage you are in. In the early stages of a particular project, you are preparing and educating yourself and getting the skills you need. Creativity can then be difficult, tedious and time-consuming. It's true that during the illumination stage (discussed in the next chapter), you experience the joy and exhilaration of opening up and catching lightning in a bottle. However, when you begin to modify, rewrite and improve your product, creativity may again appear more a curse than a blessing.

Creativity is self-expression. To the extent that you have difficulty expressing yourself and showing your individuality, creativity can be painful.

> *Good writers are generally good editors. Any serious writer will tell you that plays, novels and poems aren't just written—they're rewritten.*
> **Sheila Davis,**
> **The Craft of Lyric Writing**

> *The professional knows that careful rewriting is the difference between songs your family and friends applaud, and those that earn the applause of the whole world.*
> **Al Kasha & Joel Hirschhorn,**
> **If They Ask You, You Can Write a Song**

MYTH #7. Creativity Is Only for the Young.

There are many examples of great works being created when the creators were 'beyond their prime.' Shakespeare wrote *Hamlet* at about age 37. Newton published his *Principia Mathematica* at age 45. Copernicus was 70 when he published his *Revolution of the Heavenly Spheres.*

Creative output may decline with age, like physical stamina or memory, but there are many examples of creativity abounding into ripe old age. Picasso certainly continued his prolific activity well beyond middle age. Cervantes finished his best work, *Don Quixote*, in his fifties.

Recent psychological research found that the work quality of artists, architects and composers usually remains the same and may even improve after age sixty. The most important reason? Increased skills through continued learning. Other reasons include increased self-acceptance and more time to devote to creative pursuits.

In songwriting we have living proof that age is not a hindrance to creativity. Prolific songwriters in all styles of music, from country to rock, are forty- and fifty-something. Rock and roll was supposed to be for the under-thirty set. But Joni Mitchell, Neil Young, Carol King, Paul McCartney and Smokey Robinson continue to create good songs today.

It is important that you maintain a positive and vigorous attitude toward life to maintain your creativity. Becoming closed and rigid need not be synonymous with aging.

One of the great songwriting teams, Cynthia Weil and Barry Mann, are past fifty and still turning out great songs. These writers have honed their craft by being open to new influences in lyric content and musical composition. They keep up with the times and stay close to contemporary musical tastes. They have not sat on their laurels or allowed themselves to become rigid and inflexible.

> *a childlike man is not a man whose development has been arrested; on the contrary, he is a man who has given himself a chance of continuing to develop long after most adults have muffled themselves in the cocoon of middle age habit and convention.*
>
> **Aldous Huxley,**
> **"Vulgarity in Literature."**

MYTH #8. Creativity Is Good.

This is a very popular and sometimes tragic misconception. Good is a value judgment. What is good for one person may not be good for another. Was the creation of the atomic bomb a good thing? Are breast implants and birth control devices "good" creations? According to Existentialist Jean Paul Sartre, every act of creation is simultaneously an act of destruction. Something must "not be" in order for something else "to be."

I am also frequently amazed at how clever some thieves, murderers, stalkers, and con artists can be. Even Hannibal Lector was creative. Who can doubt the creative imagination of Michael Milken, ingenious king of the junk bond scandal?

Lawyers are particularly adept at creative interpretations of the law. By doing so they win lawsuits for their clients. Is this good or bad? Judge for yourself. Sometimes it becomes so ludicrous, it's humorous. Witness this recent lawsuit: Prisoners at Soledad Prison sued the State of California because they claimed the State was violating their civil rights. It seems that they were not being allowed conjugal visits (with wives and girlfriends). Thus, they alleged that they were being deprived of their rights to self-reproduction!

The *Los Angeles Times* on May 14, 1994, reported "Goofy Bank Robbery Story No. 4,781." A bank robber who had been sentenced to 46 months in prison is suing "the same bank he tried to rob. His claim is that his prison sentence is too long because the bank exaggerated the amount it could have lost ($27,200) had the robbery been successful . . . ."

As the Church lady from "Saturday Night Live" would say, "Now isn't that clever?"

Creative people come from all walks of life. Some of the world's greatest geniuses were not only neglectful of their families and friends, but were also batterers. In their interpersonal relationships many were sadistic, arrogant, and exploitative.

That is why this misconception is sometimes tragic. We must not only teach and nurture creativity, but we must guide it toward ends that will improve the human condition.

MYTH #9. Creative People Are Neurotic and/or Crazy.

Recent research by Paul Janos and Nancy Robinson at the University of Washington has laid this myth to rest. They found both positive psychological adjustment and maturity in personal and social growth in the gifted children they studied. Other studies with adults have confirmed that, as a group, creative individuals are not neurotic and unhealthy.

MYTH #10. Creative Geniuses Are Experts on All Topics.

Freud and Einstein once met to discuss the question "Why war?" Later, Freud commented on the momentous meeting and lack of intellectual connection by saying "He understands as much about psychology as I do about physics, so we had a very pleasant talk."

We tend to believe that people's abilities are equal across all areas of their lives. Psychologists call this the "halo effect."

The popular media reinforce the belief that individuals who achieve fame and fortune have a magical insight into all aspects of life. Most likely, this is a throwback to the primitive belief that, compared to the rest of us, creative individuals and powerful people are closer to God. We see them as partaking of divine grace, and we endow them with special vision and a clearer insight into reality. Even when we hear or read facts to the contrary, we are extremely reluctant to relinquish our beliefs. It is hard to imagine that our heroes are not so divine as we once thought.

EXERCISES AND QUESTIONS

Here are some exercises that will test your misconceptions about creativity and help you evaluate your own capacities.

1. What is your IQ? How intelligent do you believe you are? Have you ever had an IQ test? Reflect for a moment on how this knowledge affects your ability to create. How has this affected your confidence to do great works? Do you think you are not smart enough to achieve greatness?

2. Have you ever been told "you either have it or you don't?" How did it make you feel? Have you ever given up pursuing a career or hobby because you thought you "didn't have what it takes"?

3. Do you have intelligence in domains other than abstract thinking abilities? Are you "street smart" or are you an empathic person? Are you charming or particularly adept at getting others to like you? Have you used this ability to build a business, raise money, run for political office, entertain people or sell real estate?

4. On a scale from 1 to 10, rate your intrapersonal and inter-personal intelligence, spatial intelligence, musical intelligence, body and kinesthetic intelligence, linguistic intelligence and logical-mathematical intelligence.

5. Look again at the ideas of originality, fluency, flexibility and ability to elaborate. What is your strongest suit? What would it take to strengthen your weak areas?

6. Look at the different arenas in which we can be creative. Go through each and recall any experiences you had in that arena. Did you enjoy it? Were you good at it? Would you like to do it again? Why haven't you?

7. Are you intuitive? Give three examples of when you knew something was true based on your intuition. Are you or do you know of anyone who is highly creative but not in the arts or sciences? Why do you think that person is creative?

8. How is your knowledge of your particular domain keeping you back? Take a work by one of your favorite creators (an inventor, interior designer, or whatever your field of interest is) and experiment with it. Modify it. Change one aspect of it each day for a week.

9. How has age affected your creativity? Do you believe you are too old to create or that your best works are behind you? List your favorite creative persons. Beside each name, write down their ages (or your closest estimate). Write down the

name and age of the oldest creative individuals you like. How has their creativity changed with age?

10. Make a list of your favorite creative works. These could be books, houses, comedy shows, movies, sales pitches, advertising copy or whatever you are most interested in. Decide how original they are. Are they derivatives of other works? Do they fall into a genre where certain content is traditional?

11. Look at your lifestyle. How original and unique a person are you? Do something different and unusual today.

12. Visualize a creative moment in your life in which you worked, re-worked, and persevered until you got to the result that satisfied you. In your mind's eye, recall the satisfaction, joy and pleasure you experienced from that accomplishment.

13. Make a list of all your assumptions about what it takes to be a great creative person. Look carefully at each assumption and ask yourself, "Are these things true sometimes, all the time, or not at all?"

PART TWO

CREATIVE JOURNEYS: HOW TO MAKE YOUR OWN

Two roads diverged in a wood, and I—
I took the one less traveled by, and that
has made all the difference.

Robert Frost

CHAPTER 3

CATCHING LIGHTNING IN A BOTTLE

It is apparent that, to reach the breakthrough state, we must make a fundamental shift in consciously and unconsciously held beliefs we all hold about our own limitations.

Willis Harman, Ph.D., and
Howard Rheingold, authors of
Higher Creativity

Creativity is a complex, continuous activity. I've already shown that reality is in a constant state of flux. It is not made of neat and ordered parts. As we create, reality is being formed, simplified, shaped and invented. In your most intense moments you as creator, become totally absorbed in your work. You lose your sense of "me" and "it" and you may enter into a dreamlike world where you lose objectivity.

That's OK. You don't have to understand this process objectively in order to create. In fact, at the moment of greatest intensity, becoming too objective and self-conscious is totally detrimental.

Imagine a professional-league batter at the plate. He must not "think" at the moment he hits the ball. However, before that instant, he's thought about it a great deal. All the workouts, his practicing, involved mental imaging; he could see the ball as it crossed the strike zone in his mind's eye. In the same way, it's beneficial to think about the creative process objectively before you try to create. This way, you're better prepared when you do "step up to the plate."

In working with clients at my clinic, I've found it useful to break the creative process down into basic components: three levels and eight stages. The eight stages of the creative process are seen within each of the three levels: Life level, Career level and Project level. Because each lower level is nested within the level above it, be aware that you could be in one stage within one level and in a more advanced, or less advanced, stage in another level.

THE IMPORTANCE OF LEVELS

Life Level

By using the idea of levels, we can emphasize the often overlooked fact that life itself is a creative project. The "Life Level" is the context for all our activity. By examining the various stages of the creative process within the life cycle, we can better understand ebbs and flows of creativity within our lives and the changing priorities we experience as we pass through various stages.

You become involved in a specific project (writing a song, for instance), which exists within the larger context of an enterprise (writing a score for the musical theater). This work is nested inside your career as a musical composer, which, in turn, exists in the context of a full and complete life.

Career Level

Many creative individuals become fascinated early in life with a specific activity that leads them down the path of learning and discovery. If you are one of these people, you become an adventurer, a dreamer following your curiosity and learning as much as you can along the way about your object of fascination.

The singer is in love with singing, the athlete is passionate about his sport, and the entrepreneur is enchanted with launching and building a business. Whatever your passion, you dream of improving in your field, and hunger for knowledge about your domain. For whatever reason, you have answered a deep inner call to follow a particular path.

Perhaps you have no such internal compelling drive. So far, you've not found yourself, nor committed yourself to a creatively rich niche in life. If you haven't yet defined what you love, I suggest you designate that dilemma (finding a path with a heart) as your creative project. Use this book to help you find a creative solution to the riddle.

Project Level

Once you choose an arena or domain, you enter a new level within the life and career process. You begin acquiring the basic skills and knowledge of that particular sphere. If you want to write songs, you start learning about how they're put together. Without knowledge of basic song forms and musical styles, the songwriter's journey would never get off the ground. Without basic interpersonal skills, the salesman would soon lose his job.

Because of the learning that occurs on this level, you begin to master at least the essentials of your field. That is what keeps you from having to reinvent the wheel and what makes intuitive thought possible. According to Dr. Robert Glaser from the University of Pittsburgh psychology department, "At the heart of intuition is the ability to perceive large meaningful patterns."

With a thorough understanding of the territory, knowledge can be simplified and accessed more easily. Patterns emerge because information can be grouped into chunks. You begin to engage in vicarious trial-and-error learning and experimentation. In turn, this points the way to a specific solution to a creative problem.

This leads us to the eight stages of the creative process that occur at all levels.

THE EIGHT STAGES OF CREATIVITY

1. Pre-Preparation Stage—Birth of an Idea

When you, as creator, undertake a specific project, you answer another call—to a more specific undertaking. It may be a literal call, such as when the songwriter receives a phone call asking him to write a song for a recording project; or it may be the internal voice urging you to turn your life experiences into a book. The project can be as concrete as a specific assignment for pay or as ethereal as an inspirational idea or vision.

Earlier, we talked about finding work that you feel passionate about. I challenged you to use this book to find your path with a heart. If you answered that call, then at this point you should be asking yourself, *"How much do I want to find this path? How much energy do I intend to devote to this project?"*

If you've already found the work you love to do, then in the pre-preparation stage you face a specific project requiring specific solutions. For example, an interior designer is asked to solve the problem of fitting a houseful of furniture into a small apartment. To complicate matters, the client wants to upgrade her look to Country French but has only a limited budget. Or a record producer says he has a vision of his artist and wants a song that makes her sound like Mariah Carey singing "The Star Spangled Banner."

So the *call* (either literal or internal) awakens you. Now you must center on a task. If you've previously been resting complacently or scurrying around in a frantic, unfocused manner, you become goal-oriented and challenged by a desire to resolve the problem. As in choosing life's path, you must find love for your project or you'll have little energy to devote to it. Without that energy and commitment, your creation will suffer.

2. Preparation Stage—Gathering and Assessing

Chance only favors the prepared mind.
Louis Pasteur, scientist

Luck is the residue of hard work.
Branch Rickey, baseball manager

Whether your project is composing a song, developing a script, writing a book, designing a building, landscaping a yard or cooking a meal, creativity begins with thorough preparation.

You, as creator, must gather the materials and information necessary to begin. I call this the "loading up" stage. If love and desire are the key words for the pre- preparation stage, knowledge is the operative word here.

Now's the time for some research. What's been previously done by others on this type of project? Can I use what they have developed or discovered to further my own vision? What books should I read? Should I go online with my computer to seek out sources via the Internet?

Maybe your research lies closer to home—for instance, you are considering remodeling. Talking to neighbors might reveal that the former tenants of your house failed in their attempts to build a new addition because of a bad geological report, but they found an excellent architect who got around the problem. Maybe you need to contact the architect. Brainstorming with colleagues or coworkers is often useful. As I've said before, why reinvent the wheel?

When you decide on a project, either because you voluntarily chose it or because it was thrust upon you, you immediately enter into the preparation stage. One effective way to prepare for the project is to conceive of the end result during the preparation stage. Through visualization (more about this later), you can project yourself into the future and create the final product even before you begin. It doesn't have to be the actual finished product, but at least you'll have a working hypothesis, preliminary model or vision to guide your early exploration.

If you are seeking a path with a heart, ask yourself, "Do I have some vision of what my path would look like? What are the obstacles and problems I have had in trying to find a path I love?"

To organize your creative flow, it's sometimes useful to develop a mission statement and a separate vision statement. Set your goals and list the tasks to be performed. For a new enterprise, a name for the business, a site and an opening date are good organizational starting points. If you're a performer, gather the materials to be performed. Discard those that are beyond your skills. Decide which new skills you can master in a finite period of time.

For example, when I started writing this book, I looked through all the files I'd accumulated on creativity. The job was massive. I sorted these materials and tried to place them in some kind of order. Then I tried to decide what to include and what to leave out. I had so much material, it made my head swim. It was so confusing that I had to fight my inner voice (call it my "inner critic") as it undermined my desire to write the book.

"What's the use?" it said. "There's too much material. You won't be able to organize all this information and you'll wind up with a confusing, gigantic book that no one will want to publish." Still, I continued going through the materials. I was not going to let any of my old demons stop me.

My knowledge of creativity taught me that I was doing the right thing. I was preparing and confronting the chaos out of which I would create order. There was a certain amount of faith involved, but it was faith built on years of experience with the creative process. I worked through my psychic doubts and insecurities and, although those demons are still there, I've learned to deal with them better. Earlier, I might have succumbed to my inner critic. This time I was confident that I could manage my anxiety and stay focused on the writing.

I knew I could not use all the research and would have to discard much of what I had saved. Actually, I was thrilled to see that there was enough material for other books on creativity.

During this process, I remembered that an important part of creativity is knowing what not to do. In writing, an author must decide what not to say. A painter must not try to put all his images into one painting. Editing out is as significant as determining what to include. The space between notes (the so-called silences) are as much a part of the music as the sounds of notes played.

I've also experienced this preparation stage in songwriting. In writing a song, I begin by asking myself, "What's the style of this song? What's it's concept? What's its 'hook?' Will it be written for a male or female singer? Will I use complex harmonics or make it a simple three chord song?"

In any activity, a good place to begin is by asking who, what, where, when, why, and how. These are the tools a journalist uses to begin fleshing out a news story. In landscaping, you might ask, what kind of flowers you will plant, what kind of tools you will need, and when you should plant to achieve the garden of your dreams.

By asking questions and doing this preparation, you program your mind to anticipate all the details and information you'll need to create a particular project.

A key preparation technique is to reduce a large task to smaller components. Stephen Hawking, described by many as the greatest scientist of our day, addressed the difficulty in trying to think up a complete theory for the origin of the universe. Rather than grapple with the monumental task of trying to explain everything all at once, he said, "What we do instead is to look for partial theories that will describe situations in which certain interactions can be ignored or approximated in a simple manner."

Your complete preparation for the creative journey ahead not only involves gathering materials and making a plan, but also making an assessment of your supplies, talents, skills and resources. For one project, you may have to know the source for the least expensive materials for your home; in another, you may need to find your way in a labyrinthine library to get what you need.

3. First Actions Stage—Exploring

Once you've made a commitment, don't wallow in inaction. Don't fall in love with love and don't plan forever. Jump into your ship and sail off.

What you lack now you'll discover, invent or be given. You'll learn by doing. In this exploration stage you, as adventurer, must examine yourself and go through various tests and temptations. Explore various options.

Face those challengers who try to prevent you from reaching your goal. If you're not careful, you can be distracted by temptations that take you away from your destination or even destroy your mission.

It isn't all negative, though. You'll also meet advisers who will guide you toward your goal. In Chapter 6, we'll learn more about mentors and rivals, tempters and nurturers.

4. The Struggle Stage—Strategizing

The ideal passes through suffering like gold through fire.
The heavenly kingdom is attained through effort.
Fyodor Dostoevsky

Unfortunately, the road to completion is not a straight and level path. It rises and falls, and is filled with hazards, frustrations and disappointments. Your inner critic never rests. Just when you feel you've moved forward, you're threatened with total destruction. You turn a corner and your project seems to be falling apart. With no solution in sight, you temporarily meet the wall. Anxiety mounts and you may become blocked. Now's the time to take a walk or stand aside briefly to gain a fresh perspective.

This is the place to use the creativity techniques described in Chapters 8 and 9: Mind stretching, analogies, absurdiveness thinking. This will help prime your creative pump and drive you to more innovative and original solutions.

5. Incubating—Expecting

By stepping aside, you surrender to the greater wisdom of your unconscious and to the mysterious workings of the incubation stage.

Incubation is a period of dormancy where unconscious processes take over. The word incubation brings to mind a bird or a mammal resting on an egg so it can hatch. Nothing appears to be happening. Sometimes this process is just a matter of "sitting on it." Many creative people tend to panic because they fear they are being blocked. It is fear itself that often creates the block, and worrying about it creates yet another block. In this stage, free association may be linking ideas and rearranging them in unique ways.

If you've done your homework, your mind will continue working on your project even when you're not conscious of it.

Expecting that solutions will come will help them come into your consciousness.

Use your imagination to communicate with your subconscious mind. Ask it for solutions. Send it a letter requesting answers. Imagine dropping a tape in a mailbox and asking your subconscious to deliver it to you tomorrow with answers to your dilemmas. Do dream work or pray for help. Go for a walk. Distract yourself. Take a shower.

6. Illumination—Breakthrough—Birth within a Birth

> *I just hear a sound coming into my head and hope to catch it with my hands.*
> **Erroll Garner**

While reading a magazine in the doctor's waiting room or listening to the radio as you drive to work, new insights will eventually break through and reorder your project. I find that activity often stimulates ideas. I have a writer friend who says she gets some of her best solutions while she's running. The problem is she can't write them down. So, as she runs, she says them like a mantra till she gets back to her desk.

At night, just when you're trying to turn off your mind, ideas may come, seemingly unbidden. You can't stop the flow. What to do? Keep pen and paper or small tape recorder by your bed. Write them down or talk them out. In the morning, you'll see whether they're valid or not.

Don't ignore the ideas that flash through your mind. Be thankful for them. They are small flashes of light that will grow to become bigger bolts of lightning.

In any case, the pieces of the puzzle will once again fit together. One idea triggers another, and like catching lightning in a bottle you feel recharged and energized. The light bulb is aglow and you feel "high," even manic.

Congratulations, you've reached the breakthrough stage! This is the "aha" or "eureka" experience.

The Greek mathematician Archimedes is said to have yelled "Eureka" ("I found it") when he had a sudden flash of insight. In that legend, the Greek king Hiero received a crown of gold brackets. The king had no idea how valuable the crown was and could not determine how pure the gold was. He suspected that the goldsmith had used some silver instead of gold. He dropped the problem into the hands of Archimedes. The mathematician thought and thought, but no solution appeared. Finally, one day while bathing, he noticed the displacement of water caused by his body and had a sudden flash of insight. He would see if the king's crown displaced as much water as a similar amount of pure gold.

Supposedly, he jumped out of the bathtub and ran down the street naked saying, "Eureka! Eureka! I found it! I found it!"

This illumination stage is probably responsible for all our romantic notions about creativity. This is the big payoff—the most fulfilling, exciting part for creative individuals.

It can be a moment of total spontaneity, even ecstasy. At your creative peak, you feel like you've entered another world. Time is distorted. You experience a sense of happiness and well being. You've entered what is sometimes called "a state of flow" when everything seems to go perfectly. You're alive, invigorated and totally involved with what you're doing. At that moment nothing else is important and woe to anyone who intrudes on your creative process.

Athletes talk about entering "the zone." This happens, for example, when a basketball player makes one shot after another from seemingly impossible angles or distances, or where batters will see a ball gliding toward them looking as big as a beach ball.

That's the up side. The down side is that this road to Nirvana must be paid for with lots of preliminary hard work. The breakthrough experience, itself, can also be extremely frightening because it is a process of surrender and letting go.

The path to one's own heaven always leads through the voluptuousness of one's own hell.
Frederich Nietzsche

Nietzsche wasn't the only one who found surrender a frightening process. Songwriter P. F. Sloan, who penned such classics as "The Eve of Destruction," "Sins of a Family" and "Ain't No Way I'm Gonna Change My Mind," describes one night of ecstasy and torment: "I was up most of that night battling. I don't know who I was battling or what, but I vividly recall saying to some higher music power, 'Please let me be released from this. Please let me get it out. Let me be released . . . .'"

In his story, a voice kept saying, "No, no, sorry, you've got to live with it. Can't let you fall on this one."

"Finally," he says, "words would start to come and I would see them and I would be filled with tears of joy, and I would be so happy that they were being given."

Suspending judgmental consciousness is essential to this moment of illumination. You must open the doors to the free flow of energy. You have to stand aside and not get in your own way. You must surrender to the greater creative force within.

Creative people talk about going beyond themselves at moments of great creativity and of doing more than they knew how to do.

In the *Los Angeles Times Magazine,* September 2, 1990, Garcia Marquez reports being perplexed by the mystery of how writing begins somewhat mechanically but then, "There arrives a moment at which you have such an identification with the subject that it carries you away and the words begin to come out on their own."

7. Verification Stage—Polishing and Refining

The verification stage could be called the rewriting, reworking, polishing or "tying up loose ends" stage. The word verification may be more appropriate for the sciences, mathematics and the "thinking professions." Polishing and refining better describes this stage in other creative fields.

During the previous illumination stage, the best strategy was to suspend the critic and let the child within you come forth. Ideas were allowed to flow freely. You didn't want to inhibit or restrict yourself. It was important to allow things to just happen. You needed to suspend the perfectionistic tendencies that led to premature judgment and self doubts.

Now that you've done your homework, had a flash of insight or a bolt of lightning and poured new ideas into a product, you need to go back and take an objective, detached perusal. This is the time to look at your project from a detailed and critical point of view.

"How are others going to perceive this?" "How good is this work?" "How can I improve it?" This is the time to fine-tune your effort by asking yourself tough questions. If you're in business, this is the time to ready the product for market. You must give it a rigorous going-over before taking it out into the world.

8. Celebration

Mission accomplished! You finished the project. It's time for congratulations. Take time to enjoy the feeling of accomplishment. Thank others for their help and praise their accomplishments. Enjoy yourself and your sense of competence.

Epilogue

This might even be called the ninth stage because it often occurs after the celebration stage. "If I'm so great, why do I feel depressed now?" you may ask yourself. Call it the hangover, post-partum depression, the 'empty nest' syndrome, 'buyer's regret' or whatever, but there is often a let-down feeling after you complete a project. As author John Cheever put it, "One not only writes a book. One lives it. Upon completing it there are certain symptoms of death."

Don't worry. This is a normal reaction. Wallow in it for awhile, but not for too long. Your next creative adventure may be just moments away.

EXERCISES

In Chapter 1 we discussed an everyday exercise program. In addition, try some of these:

★ 1. Write down five things you love to do. Would you do them for a long period of time or even without being paid? Do several of these things have a common link? Could you build this into a career? When was the last time you engaged in one of these activities?

★ 2. Write down your best skills. Rate them from 1 to 3 in terms of how much you love to exercise these skills.

★ 3. Take out your resume. Look it over. Do all your creative skills show up on your resume? Why not?

★ 4. Recall your last creative project. How did you get involved in it? Where did "the call" come from, yourself or someone else? Did you feel challenged? Did you do it to solve a problem or because you had an inspired vision for something you wanted to create?

★ 5. Make a list of at least ten negative, discouraging comments you hear from your inner critic. Can you identify where each of these originated? Was it a parent . . . a teacher? Visualize the interaction and feel the emotions you felt then. Take a deep breath, relax, say "I am a very creative person" and move on.

★ 6. As part of your preparation stage, next time you begin a project, ask who, what, where, when, how and why.

★ 7. Recall when you last had an "aha" experience. Or maybe it was "that's it" or "wow" or "got it!" How often have you been at the end of your rope and ready to quit when you finally broke through? How often have you been in a slump, depressed and/or frustrated, and then suddenly came up with a solution? How do you react to slumps?

★ 8. Visualize "hitting the wall"—that moment when you feel totally blocked and can't go farther. Draw it or paint it. Fantasize about how you would deal with it. Would you scale it, break it or go around it?

★   9. If you're creating a product, ask yourself, "Will I market my product? How? Where? Will I get others to do it or will I do it myself?" Have you ever done a marketing plan? Read one or more of the following books listed in the bibliography: *Guerilla Marketing*, by Jay Conrad Levinson; *How to Get Rich in Mail Order* by Melvin Powers; or *1001 Ways to Market Your Books*, by John Kremer.

★ 10. Do you like to be praised for your work? Recall a moment when you were being congratulated for a mission accomplished. How did it feel? Would you like to feel that way again? Make a plan to make it happen again.

CHAPTER 4

WHAT'S YOUR PERSONALITY?
TRAITS AND TYPES

Of all the characteristics of well-known creative people, independence and passion are the ones that appear most consistently across different fields and through different generations.
Teresa Amabile, *The Social Psychology of Creativity*

I have no special gift—I am only passionately curious.
**Albert Einstein in P. Schlipps,
*Albert Einstein: Philosopher-scientist,
Library of Living Philosophers***

Ralph, the office manager of a large corporation, was giving me a tour of the corporate offices. When we came to the "Creative Department," he matter-of-factly turned to me and said, "This is where we keep the creative types. You know the ones that dress weird and are always looking off into space."

On another occasion, I eavesdropped on a small group of women at a well-known Los Angeles restaurant. They were checking-out men by trying to guess their professions. I was intrigued by their game. "He's not the creative type," said one when referring to a man dressed in a conservative suit. "He looks more like an executive than an artist."

These examples show a few stereotypes we have about creative people—about what they look like and how they behave. In fact, there is a common belief that creative people fit a certain personality type. How often have you heard someone say, "I'm just not the creative type"?

But *is* there a creative personality type? In this chapter, we debunk what is probably the eleventh myth about creativity. There is no single creative personality type. Instead, there are many creative personality types, each creative in a specific way.

Do creative people have certain personality traits? Are there attitudes or behaviors that do not form a whole personality style but are better to have than others? As we shall see, there are no universally "good" traits. A trait, even when it is helpful for the creative process, is not useful in every phase of creativity.

THE CHILD WITHIN

Creativity is a magical process whether it is seen in art, science or in everyday life. It involves a spontaneous flow of inventiveness and ingenuity in which reality takes on new meanings and manifestations. It is a return to the playful child within us.

A child comes into the world full of wonder and amazement. Every day is a new experience. As the child grows, it creates and re-creates itself. The child's mind is fluid, flexible and flowing. As the personality is shaped, however, the ability to be flexible and to see the world in unique ways becomes closed. As we mature, some of us become more closed than others, and a few do preserve the child's imagination.

Are openness, flexibility and curiosity traits that creative individuals carry over into adult life?

CREATIVE TRAITS

For years, researchers have tried to identify common personality traits of creative individuals. Let's look at the results.

Frank Barron, a prominent psychologist in creativity research, obtained information on a variety of creative persons. He studied professionals from architects to military officers. Following is a list of adjectives commonly used by professionals to describe their most creative peers: flexible, unconventional, intuitive, courageous, perceptive, uninhibited, original, moody, ingenious, self-centered, dedicated, self-assertive, hardworking, dominant, persistent, eccentric, and independent.

The respondents rated *courageous* along with *self-confident* and *dominant* as the most important characteristics of creative people.

Psychologist Rollo May, in *The Courage to Create*, also rates courage as essential to creativity. It takes courage to say or do or make something different. Only the brave risk being rejected, laughed at or labeled dumb.

R. B. Cattell, developer of the Sixteen Personality Factor Questionnaire (16PF), tested Olympic athletes and scientific researchers on 16 different dimensions. These groups scored low on the Guilt Proneness (O) scale and high on Dominance (E). I take this to mean that these successful and creative individuals were competitive and assertive. What's more, they didn't apologize for it!

> *Geniuses are not meek, submissive souls.*
> **Dean Keith Simonton, *Greatness***

Now, look back at the list of characteristics of creative people. Just as we saw in Chapter 2, intelligence is not even included as an important characteristic. But courage, self-confidence, and dominance are.

CREATIVE ROLES

Roger Von Oech, author of *A Kick in the Seat of the Pants*, has an interesting and amusing way of looking at the personality traits of creative people. He describes four roles (the explorer, the artist, the judge and the warrior) played by the creative person. Then he discusses the importance of each of these four roles during different stages of the creative process. In a sense, the creative person wears different hats at different stages of creative activity. The Explorer is always searching for new information while the Artist turns this information into new ideas. The Judge evaluates the merits of an idea and, finally, the Warrior carries the idea into action.

The Explorer

The Explorer is always looking for adventure and tries to investigate new frontiers. His hunger for discovery overcomes his fear of the unknown. This role is most important in the preparation stage of creativity. As an explorer, you are *curious* and *open*. You take risks in searching and exploring new territory. Columbus took the risk of falling off the face of the earth. Ulysses ventured into the far waters of the Mediterranean under peril of encountering aliens, sea monsters or boiling water.

In this role, you are constantly searching for new opportunities to be creative. You see problems as challenges. Everyday situations become material for whatever projects you are working on. While others are numb or insensitive to the usual, or fail to see the extraordinary in the ordinary, the Explorer searches with the expectation of finding the pearl in the oyster. As the Explorer, you are an adventurer who is always on the lookout for the "New World."

The Artist

The second role Van Oech discusses is the Artist. The Artist transforms information into new ideas. As the Artist, you are *flexible, open, persistent* and *imaginative.* You trust your intuition and believe yourself to be creative. The Artist is always changing and modifying things. You, the Artist, can tolerate ambiguity and chaos. While wearing this hat, you are more prone to experiment, fool around and modify, modify, and modify. You also know how to do nothing (incubate). You become like a child at play, unconventional and uninhibited.

The Judge

The role of critic and evaluator is left to the Judge. Remember how, in Chapter 3, we talked about the importance of not judging our ideas during the illumination phase? We saw that the inner critic can be stifling and that we need to learn how to control him\her. In the verification (or the polishing and refining) stage, however, we need to be critical. As Judge, we provide constructive criticism and ensure that our product is worth defending. It is at this point that the traits of *perfectionism* and *good critical thinking* are particularly important.

The Judge also plays an important role in protecting the Warrior, the last role defined by Van Oech.

The Warrior

The Warrior carries your idea into action. Here, you take your products to market and try to convince others as to the value of your creation. You are both soldier and salesperson. The Warrior must be *persistent, self-confident* and *courageous.* By honing and polishing the product, the Judge protects the Warrior in you. Because you know your product is worth defending, you are less vulnerable to rejection and ridicule. To be competitive and reach success, you must be bold.

CREATIVE PERSONALITY TYPES

So far we have discussed various traits that are characteristic of creative persons. We have seen that a particular trait is more or less important depending on what phase of creative process you are in. Now we ask: Is there a constellation of personality traits that is common to all creative individuals? In other words, is there a creative personality type? Are you that type?

First, let's define what we mean by personality type or style. As a child develops, he tries out various coping strategies and behaviors for dealing with the environment. These strategies and behaviors meet with varying degrees of success and satisfaction in obtaining desired goals. From these behaviors, the child develops preferred patterns of coping which then become ingrained through repetition and reinforcement. These patterns of attitudes, habits, and emotions become the traits which characterize your personality style or type.

There are several systems for classifying and describing personality types. One that is widely used in clinical practice is contained in the American Psychiatric Diagnostic Manual known as DSM IVR.

Using this personality classification system, Anthony Storr in *The Dynamics of Creation,* looks at schizoid, obsessive-compulsive and manic-depressive personality types and their relationship to creativity. I have added my observations about histrionic, narcissistic and authoritarian personality types and arrived at some conclusions regarding the relationship between creativity and personality.

Psychologists who use the DSM-IVR system describe people according to these personality types. Usually people don't fall neatly into this categories. Instead, most individuals are a combination of these "pure" types. Is one of these types more creative than the others? Are some of them not creative at all?

▓ *Schizoid Personality*

The schizoid personality type is characterized by detachment and emotional isolation. He is a loner and has difficulty bonding with others. He may appear cold and aloof and disinterested in intimacy. Storr sees these character traits in such creative geniuses as Einstein, Kafka and Newton. They were able to spend long periods in solitude thinking about complex, abstract problems. In other words, they put their schizoid detachment to creative use. In the case of Einstein, he performed mental experiments and seemed to prefer them to real life experimentations. He is quoted as saying ". . . much of what we learned from the sense of touch was unscientific prejudice, which must be rejected if we are to have a true picture of the world."

Einstein's creativity was partly motivated by a desire to escape ordinary life. He easily withdrew into himself and often showed little appreciation for social discourse. During a conversation, he was known to ". . . fall silent and stop listening to you. He would rise to his feet without a word, or remain sitting motionless. The effect would be the same. He would be unreachable . . . ." Clearly being schizoid did not interfere with his creativity. But is a schizoid personality essential to high levels of creativity?

Histrionic Personality

The histrionic personality type is characterized by a flare for the dramatic. Histrionic people love to be on stage and attract attention. Their seductive and manipulative maneuvers are designed to obtain love and attention. This constant need for admiration and esteem from others leads them to exaggeration and flamboyant behavior. They are skilled at getting attention focused on them since they are extroverted, exhibitionistic and imaginative. They love to use provocative subjects such as sex to draw attention to themselves. Histrionic people are often perceived as fickle and flighty.

You can see from the above description that histrionic personalities are particularly suited for a life as entertainment professionals. They have vivid imaginations. This, and their talent for getting others to like them, serve them well in their roles as performers. They are well represented in the world of actors, singers, and dancers.

Narcissistic Personality

Narcissistic personality types are also charming and talented in getting others to like them. Although the narcissist shares the charm and charisma of the histrionic personality, the narcissist is more interested in manipulating others for purposes of exploitation. He needs to be liked and admired. This is not so much an attempt to feel worthwhile and loved, but to use these affectionate bonds to exploit and obtain superiority over others. The narcissist feels more self-sufficient and is more independent than the histrionic person. He doesn't need others; he only uses them to satisfy his power needs. The narcissist is arrogant and harbors feelings of deep hostility and disdain for others. He believes himself superior to others and, like the histrionic personality, has a vivid imagination. He is so convinced of his superior worth that he believes others should feel honored to be in his company. His self-confidence and arrogance often cause others to admire and obey him. He is a prime candidate for what we will later call a "psychic vampire."

Narcissists are not confined to the world of entertainment. Among well-known narcissists, we must include military conquerors such as Napoleon and Hitler.

▒ *Manic-Depressive Personality*

Although not technically a personality style according to the DSM IVR, I will include manic-depressives as part of this discussion. I think this is warranted since creative persons are often associated with this psychological disorder. Manic-depressives suffer from extreme mood swings. They often ride a roller coaster of emotions ranging from depression to mania (high energy states). When they are depressed, they fear losing love and become dependent. In the manic phase, they can become ruthless and self-seeking. We then see a tremendous surge in energy and a consequent increase in creative output. The list of great artists who have suffered from this disorder is widely known and includes famous painters such as Michelangelo, Van Gogh and Raphael; composer Robert Schumann among others; and writers such as Edgar Allen Poe. In fact, it is this syndrome that has led to the popular myth that geniuses are somehow crazy or prone to mental illness!

▒ *Obsessive-Compulsive Personality*

> *The most idealistic presidents were frequently the most inflexible . . .*
> **Dean Keith Simonton**

The obsessive-compulsive's most predominant feature is his rigidity and need to control. He is given to obsessing about details, tidiness and cleanliness. Obsessive-compulsives do not easily tolerate disorder and they often engage in compulsive, ritualistic behaviors such as constantly washing their hands or checking and rechecking work already completed. They have difficulty letting go and taking risks.

Storr points out that many creative people display this personality style in their creative work. He cites the great classical composer Stravinsky and his need for symmetry and regularity as examples of this. One biographer writes that Stravinsky was meticulously obsessed with details. His writing desk was covered with bottles of different colored inks "each having its purpose, its meaning, its special use: one for the notes, another the text, a third the translation; one for title, another for the musical directions; meanwhile the bar lines were ruled, and the mistakes carefully erased." He also used various types of india rubbers as well as all sorts of rulers, erasers, pen knives, and other instruments.

A description by Roman painter De Sanctis of the famous composer Rossini is equally revealing: "Another thing that I observed about him was the regularity of his habits, not to mention the symmetrical order in which he placed the furniture and objects around him . . . which did not give the notion of a room lived in by an artist, whom we more easily imagine inclined to disorder. When, struck by that perfect orderliness, I showed my surprise to the Maestro, he said to me: 'Eh, my dear fellow, order is wealth'."

CONFORMITY AND AUTHORITARIANISM

Before we reach our conclusions regarding a creative personality type, let's contrast it with its opposite. In other words, let's see what a creative person is not.

Two researchers, Adorno and Frankel-Brunswick, studied authoritarian, rigid individuals. In many respects, this authoritarian personality type is the opposite of what Frank Barron has described as the creative personality. Authoritarians are closed-minded, dependent and, like the obsessive-compulsive, have a low tolerance for ambiguity. They follow the "herd mentality" and have a strong need to conform in order to feel secure. Authoritarians fear their own freedom of choice and are bound by strict adherence to traditions and institutions. This description reminds me of racists and bigots, as well as members of fundamentalist religious groups and cults.

But are these authoritarian types really less creative than other personality types? In spite of the work of these researchers, I'm not sure that we can conclude that authoritarian personalities are non-creative. I have seen many creative people who are rigid and authoritarian and sometimes even sadistic and cruel. They are sometimes creative in spite of their authoritarian nature or, possibly, because of it.

When we discussed Van Oech's classification of traits and stages, we saw how different traits are important at different stages of the creative process. Authoritarian traits may be very useful in the Warrior stage when persistence and even stubbornness may be useful. Sometimes an unyielding and rigid stance can convince and persuade others who may be closed to innovation and change. In addition, a product created by an authoritarian person may find its greatest success in an authoritarian society. A conservative product, even if it is full of sadism and cruelty, may be just what an authoritarian audience wants. But that's another story.

Robert Weisberg in *Creativity: Beyond the myth of Genius*, points out that many esteemed and creative scientists were very stubborn and inflexible individuals. They weren't open to new information in their search for "truth." Instead, they were very closed and "strongly committed to proving cherished hypotheses." They weren't really objectively searching for truth, but were out to prove how right they were.

> *On the average, those rated as the greatest chief executives*
> *of American history are those at either extreme—the very*
> *dogmatic and the very non-dogmatic.*
> **Dean Keith Simonton**

The authoritarian personality type, then, can be a creative type and the same is true for the other personality types. Some creative individuals are very insecure and have low self-esteem. Others are paranoid, histrionic or passive-aggressive.

CONCLUSION

My conclusion? There is no *one* creative personality type. Each type has certain strengths and certain weaknesses. Your strengths and weaknesses will show up at different stages of the creative process. More important, however, it is the way you use your resources that will determine the kinds of creative pursuits you engage in. It will color the content and style of your creations. Since your personality type is your style and manner of relating to the world, it is itself a creative work. It comes about by your constant interaction with the environment. Your personality type is formed by the thousands, if not millions of choices you make. These choices make up your values and preferences, coloring all your relations with the world.

Specific attitudes and traits are useful in one creativity stage but destructive in another. A creative individual balances these attitudes and understands when it is appropriate and fruitful to behave in one way and not another. This is the lesson to be learned from our study of personality traits and types. Creativity is the process of struggling with your feelings, attitudes and behaviors to maximize productivity. It is in this struggle that you are a creative and heroic figure. In overcoming your demons, you create and re-create yourself. You are reborn with each new creation. You shed your old self just like a snake sheds its old skin.

The creative act itself is a dynamic interplay of opposing forces that, when resolved or synthesized, produces a novel ideal or product. That is why the creative person is a paradox of contra-dictory attitudes and is in a constant struggle to balance these opposing forces. It is this integration and resolution of opposites that produces the energy and material for creative works.

The creative personality is best characterized, then, by an ability to maintain inconsistent views and to struggle with the tension of opposing psychic forces.

Your single most important asset as a creative person, however, is your determination to change what you have already learned. Do not be satisfied with learning a domain. Change it. Constantly experiment and play around with the material. Add and modify. Get used to living in a world of constant motion. Create a world that is fluid because of your creative interactions with it. Be absorbed with your work like a lover obsessed with the beloved.

> *The most crucial factor in creativity is the motivation to do something creative.*
>
> Teresa Amabile,
> *The Social Psychology of Creativity*

> *'Personality' characteristics of genius have no content; they are basically motivational in nature.*
>
> Robert Weisberg, *Creativity: Beyond the Myth of Genius*

EXERCISES

Here are some exercises to work on, or rather, play with. And the next time someone asks if you are the creative type, confidently answer, "Sure I am!" Erase that negative program that says "I'm not the creative type." Replace it with "I create in my own way."

1. How curious are you? Are you open and adventurous? Do you fear the unknown or look at it as a challenge? Rate yourself on a scale from 1 to 10.

2. When was the last time you were assertive or even aggressive? Would you describe yourself as an introvert or as an extrovert? Write a story about how you see yourself.

3. How flexible and imaginative are you? Rate yourself on a scale from 1 to 10. Do you always like things to be neat and orderly? Do you get anxious when things are not tidy and in their place? Rate your tolerance for ambiguity on a scale from 1 to 10.

4. When was the last time you did something unconventional? When was the last time you acted childish or silly? Imagine yourself fully involved in child's play. On a scale from 1 to 10 rate your ability to play like a child.

5. Rate your Judge on a scale from 1 to 10. Do you use self-criticism to improve yourself? Do you rewrite and rewrite or work and rework your project until it is perfect, or do you hate to change anything once you've done it?

6. Rate your Warrior on a scale of 1 to 10. How good are you at accepting rejection? How confident and persistent are you in marketing your ideas and projects?

7. Are you particularly good at manipulating others and getting them to like you? Are you doing it because you need to feel loved or because you want to exploit them or victimize them? Are you charismatic? Review your interpersonal interactions and look at those dynamics. Make a list of things you would like to change in your interpersonal behavior.

8. Do you prefer being alone or with others? Are you moody? How does this affect your creativity? Do you have bursts of energy where you become extremely productive? Schedule some time each week for being along. If you suffer from severe mood swings and are not presently getting professional help, consider doing so.

9. How ambitious are you? Do you have an overwhelming desire to succeed? Do you feel you love your work?

10. How well do you tolerate tension? When you are confronted with obstacles and tensions, do you enjoy the challenge? Are you persistent? Do you get up when you are down or do you give up easily?

11. Would you like to be a champion? Do you identify with successful individuals in your field? Why not? Are they more creative than you? What made them more successful than you?

 12. Are you afraid of risking being ridiculed or being laughed at? Do you avoid asking questions for fear that your peers will think you are asking dumb questions? Do you fear making mistakes so much that you don't take risks or that you keep a rigid routine?

CHAPTER 5

ROADBLOCKS AND BLOCK BUSTERS

Genius, in truth, means little more than the faculty of perceiving in an unhabitual way.
William James

"What can I do when I get blocked? How can I get unblocked?" I am repeatedly asked these questions during my creativity workshops. Similarly, I am asked about ruts and slumps which are blocks by different names. In this chapter, I discuss some of the biggest blocks to creativity and what to do about them.

What is a block? If creativity is letting things flow, then blocking is getting stuck. We may be fixed in a habitual pattern or fixated on an unsolvable problem. Blocking becomes evident when we run out of fresh ideas or don't seem to make any progress on our projects.

When we block, we lose our desire to be creative and resort to familiar escapes. We veg in front of the TV, go shopping at the mall or clean the house from top to bottom. In severe cases, we may engage in self-destructive behavior such as excessive drinking or taking drugs.

Blocks manifest themselves in procrastination and lack of productivity. Blocks cause negative emotions such as frustration, shame, guilt, anger, jealousy and feelings of failure.

Many of my workshop attendees report that they often procrastinate. They are easily distracted or avoid being "creative" whenever possible. Just as they are about to start their creative projects, they suddenly become aware of distractions and other things they just "have to do." An infinite number of obstacles get in the way of their commitment to creativity. Just before their scheduled time to work, they have to vacuum, locate their eyeglasses or find the proper writing paper. They have to clean the garage or make this or that phone call. It's amazing how creative a procrastinator can be in finding ways to avoid being creative!

Even the great creators procrastinate. Garcia Marquez, the renowned Latin American writer, says he looks for pretexts to avoid writing. He reads the newspaper, makes phone calls and rejoices when the electricity goes out and the computer goes down! In a *Los Angeles Times Magazine* article, September 2, 1990, Marquez states that even what he wears can be an excuse to procrastinate. He arrives late at his desk and uses the excuse that he doesn't have anything to wear. He can't even decide what pair of pants to put on to match the shirt he is wearing. "I have a closet full of clothes, and I scream, 'I don't have anything to wear.' Of course, all of this is a pretext because of the fear of going to write."

What creates these blocks? Are they inevitable or can they be avoided?

As I began writing this chapter, I realized that my whole book deals with blocks. Misconceptions, fears, attitudes, environmental obstacles and lack of specific problem-solving techniques cause blocks. Practically every chapter of this book is about a type of block.

So as we talk about the various causes of blocks, I'll refer you to sections in this book that deal with that particular issue in more detail. The number of ways you can block is probably countless. This is not intended to be an exhaustive list of blocks. It covers only those I consider to be the most important.

LIMITED OR RESTRICTED DEFINITION
OF CREATIVITY

In the first chapter, I showed how we are all creative, all the time. Remember that creativity is the essence of being part of a dynamic universe. We can't help but be creative. We are part of an energy system that is constantly manifesting itself in new forms. I personally find it reassuring and liberating to know that I am partaking in a larger, creative, cosmic process and that I am an expression of this universal creative energy.

Some people have a very restricted view of creativity. They think they are being creative only when they produce tangible products that are valued by others or by society. No wonder they have a problem with their creativity! If you had such a definition of creativity, you would feel noncreative most of the time.

Read over Chapter 1 and reframe the problem of dealing with this type of block. The issue is not whether you are creative. Rather, the problem may be how original or prolific you are. Or it may be that you are having difficulty producing in a specific domain. You think that you are blocked, but most likely you are engaged in creative activity in some other domain. Perhaps you are in the kitchen creating a very interesting meal or you are rearranging your schedule so you can take one of your sons to the baseball game and see a movie, too. If you reframe the situation, you see that you are being creative in another area and not blocked at all. (Part II of this book deals in greater detail with reframing and refocusing your energy.)

But then there are those times when your energy is not flowing and you are not actively involved in your chosen project. You are not flowing as an artist or as a parent or as an executive. What keeps you from these objects of desire? What keeps you from committing yourself to this creative activity?

MISTAKING THE INCUBATION STAGE FOR BLOCKING

In Chapter 3 we talked about the incubation stage of the creative process and its potential pitfalls. During this stage you are not creating anything dramatically new. You are in a period of dormancy. Nothing appears to be happening, and you may become frustrated or frightened when nothing happens. You may panic or become distracted. Don't. Remind yourself that you are waiting for your egg to hatch. Imagine yourself completing your project or intentionally distract yourself in some pleasurable way. Remember, fears and anxieties create blocks. Facing our fears and anxieties unleashes our creative flow.

FEARS

There are many fears that cause us to block. Here is an overview of the most common ones. In Chapters 9 and 10, I discuss specific solutions to overcoming these fears.

A particularly paralyzing fear is the *fear of failure*. This is the fear that once you get into a particular project and start creating, it won't be very good. You think you'll be very disappointed with the results. You imagine that people will say, "How dumb!"or "This is amateurish" or that it is not a quality product. This fear will nag you until it undermines your project, if you let it. Remember, creativity involves taking the risk of being rejected.

The fear of failure may also rear its ugly head and manifest in incomplete projects or in haphazard endings. We stop just short of success because we fear completing our project and putting it up to the competition. Our fear of failure is more powerful than our desire for success. We may fear that, if we fail, we will be ridiculed and humiliated. Perhaps we were victims of ridicule as children and we fear reliving that horrible experience.

When Jay, a client of mine, was in grade school, his teacher ridiculed him for writing a poem that she considered childish. Apparently, she was put off because Jay's poem was about a talking rabbit. Jay stopped writing poetry until we uncovered the source of his block and worked through it. In thinking about this teacher, I was just glad she didn't have Walt Disney in her classroom. She might have ruined his creativity and the world would have been a sadder place for it. Such is the power of the teaching profession.

Our projects often will not live up to the expectations we had in the preparation stage. We shoot for the stars and reach the moon. That's OK, but watch out for your inner critic. If you let him, he will undermine your efforts with such thoughts as "Eh, it's not very original." One result of this is that you may then be left with a lack of commitment in fine tuning your product. For instance, the salesperson who is suffering from fear of failure will rush when making a presentation and may rationalize her behavior by saying, "It's only a proposal."

A second fear that blocks our creative flow is *fear of problems.* When we define something as a "problem," we tend to worry about it. We tense up and feel like we can't deal with it. Or we avoid it altogether. We see it as a problem rather than as an opportunity and a challenge. The avoidance of a problem may bring temporary relief, but in the long run, avoidance leads to feelings of meaninglessness, emptiness and superficiality. And blocked creativity.

To avoid thinking about something is known as repression. It is the behavior of "not thinking" or avoiding certain thoughts. Avoidance leads to bottled-up emotions and, consequently, negative attitudes. Unrecognized feelings such as anger and jealousy get displaced onto others, particularly our loved ones. When we can't admit that we have these emotions, we project them onto the world. The world is now seen as hostile and menacing and our creative flow is compromised or, at best, distorted.

Fear of work is a third major fear. Earlier, I pointed out that creativity consists of 99 percent perspiration and 1 percent inspiration. It often involves a lot of time and effort. We must dedicate a great deal of time to learning a craft, and we must exert a great deal of effort doing and redoing our creation until it is satisfactory or even excellent.

Without the commitment to hard work, our projects will be condemned to mediocrity. Often our best works arrive on the other side of despair. If we can persist against the wall of doubt and despair, we will go beyond the good work to arrive at the truly great uniqueness within.

Fear of fun is an opposite but equally destructive fear. Some people are brought up to think that fun is a waste of time, evil or childish. In actuality, the most innovative solutions are often found when you are playing or fooling around. This is because humor and laughter loosen up material from the unconscious mind. They allow us to suspend logic long enough for novel perceptions to break through. (See Chapter 10 for a discussion of humor, play and fun in the creative process.)

Overcome your *fear of exploring.* Creativity involves experimentation. Exploration and curiosity lead you into areas beyond your knowledge and experience. Fear of the unknown cuts you off from the endless possibilities of your imagination. Some people always need to know where they are going. They don't want to explore or venture off the beaten path. Creativity means exploring new directions and changing things. Rigid people like things to stay the same.

According to biographer Pierre Daix, Picasso had ". . . a compulsion to experiment—to try out varied compositional arrangements, to draw the same object from diverse angles, and to capture contrasting emotions, including ones that were highly evocative and dramatic."

Look out for the *fear of abandonment.* This is especially true for women and minorities. Fear of abandonment makes it more difficult to take risks. It is the fear that if you don't conform and you stand out you may be seen as uppity or arrogant. The fear is that you will fall flat on your face and end up alone and shipwrecked.

For those of us born in poverty, the risks inherent in being creative may be very great. It is sometimes easier to follow the sure thing and guarantee ourselves some measure of material success, even if it means giving up our talents or our unique perceptions. The result, however, can be a life filled with bitterness and cynicism in spite of material success.

Fear of being alone is the seventh fear that blocks creative flow. Many creative people like solitude. In their solitude, they find a time to pursue their passions. By contrast, some people cannot put up with solitude for very long. After a few minutes and, certainly after a few hours, they start to feel depressed, bored, nervous or confused. They are unable to coordinate their thoughts, feelings and actions in orderly ways. To keep from feeling unhappy or bored, they pick up a telephone or turn on the television.

ANXIETY

Anxiety is just as deadly to creativity as fear. There are many situations that can cause anxiety. Disorder, for example, may precipitate it. Some people like things to be very ordered and clear and when things are disorderly or ambiguous, they become anxious and nervous. If they are unable to tolerate these emotions, they end up avoiding these situations. At best, they tense up and shut down their imaginations.

By its nature, however, creativity means reorganizing and having things "not clear." It involves change. Not knowing which direction things are going to take or what the outcome of an activity will be is central to the creative process. We have to be able to tolerate a certain amount of ambiguity and disorder, at least in certain stages of the creative process.

Anxiety clouds the mind. It contributes to blocks in problem-solving and restricts access to the vast creative reservoir of the unconscious. It often leads to finishing a project too quickly in order to get it over with. If, because of our anxiety, we began judging our ideas too soon, we may restrict the quantity and quality of our work. We may thus suffer from what I fondly call *premature evaluation.*

Learning to identify when you become anxious is a first step. Relaxation techniques can then be practiced to replace anxiety with calmness and openness. See Chapters 7 and 8 for self-programming techniques that can help you control anxiety.

NEGATIVE SELF-CONCEPT

A negative self-concept is a self-fulfilling prophesy. If you believe you are no good, that you are not creative and never will be, then of course you will very likely be unsuccessful.

The inner critic is the inner voice that can stifle our productive impulses. Dealing with the inner critic is one of the most important tasks and challenges that the creative individual faces. It is the most important relationship that the creator confronts. Depending on how you deal with your inner critic, your creative process will flourish or die. The inner critic is neither friend nor foe, it is both.

Chapters 7 and 8 explore the use of Neuro Linguistic Programming and visualization techniques for building a strong self-image and learning to expect creative and productive behaviors from ourselves.

PERFECTIONISM

Perfectionism is often cited as a major obstacle to creativity. In Chapter 4 we explored personality traits and asked whether some personality traits are more conducive to creative activity and whether perfectionism is a bad trait.

The fact is that perfectionism is a trait of many creative people. This perfectionistic attitude is what helps them strive toward creating something of high quality. Perfectionism can be a wonderful trait to have in the verification stage, for example, where we critique our work and fine-tune it. This is the hard work required to raise the quality of the product.

I have known many creative people who were very perfectionistic. I have been impressed by the gardener who creates a beautifully landscaped garden and works on it until it is perfect. I have admired the wallpaper hanger who wants perfection in his masterpiece. I have also observed that, once they have created something they feel is perfect, they will stand firm and stand ready to defend the quality of their creations. They work toward that perfection. That is where the 99 percent perspiration comes in.

Perfectionism, on the other hand, can be counterproductive when it stifles curiosity and creates fear. It is detrimental when perfectionism makes you afraid to do anything because you want it to be perfect. It is a block when it prevents you from opening up to new experiences. It is an obstacle when it prevents you from letting things come out because, before they come out, you want them to be already perfect. In these instances perfectionism is killing your creativity.

This is especially true if you are in the illumination stage of creativity where you are better off letting ideas flow out and suspending the inner critic. Coupled with anxiety, perfectionism can suppress the quantity and quality of creative ideas.

JEALOUSY, ENVY AND REPRESSED RAGE

You now know that avoiding problems and hard work can lead to feelings of frustration and anger. If we are not being true to our inner needs or not living out our own values, we can become alienated. We then live for others and according to *their* plans. If we lack commitment to our values and lose faith in ourselves, we become lost souls. Jealousy, envy and rage are the result. These are major creativity spoilers. Chapter 10 deals with these and related issues.

ENVIRONMENTAL BLOCKS

Human ecology includes the physical, social and economic environments. You need to decide what creative environment is conducive to doing your work. What works for someone else may not work for you. For example, many people cannot concentrate with background music or noise. You, on the other hand, may be most creative under these conditions. Mozart loved to compose his music in his head while he enjoyed the quietness of a carriage ride. But when he got ready to write it down on paper, he preferred the energy and stimulation of a party in which to work.

Your creative sphere also includes your economic environment. If you are too exhausted from your "day job" to do any creative work at night, you may need to reset your priorities. Perhaps you could get by with less money or by decreasing your material wants.

Surround yourself with friends and relationships who support your creativity. Avoid people who drain your psychic energy! Find mentors and counselors who align themselves with your goals and objectives. (See chapter 6 for a more thorough discussion of maximizing your creative environment.)

LACK OF CRAFT OR TECHNIQUES

Apprenticeships were the most common way of learning a craft in medieval Europe. Today there are diverse institutions of learning and self-help books. There is no right way of obtaining knowledge of the domain in which you want to be creative. And there are no excuses for not having that knowledge.

One of the best ways of learning your craft is through imitation and analysis. Study the works of others you admire. The greatest creators became absorbed in the works of their colleagues and predecessors. As Einstein said, "They stood on the shoulders of giants." You too should strive to stand on the shoulders of giants.

Besides craft, there are specific problem-solving techniques to help make the mind more flexible. Without the proper tools, a carpenter cannot build a house no matter how much desire or motivation he might have. Without knowledge of spices, it is impossible to be a good gourmet cook.

OTHER SOURCES OF BLOCKS

The number of blocks is innumerable and we have just reviewed the most important ones. Other more serious sources of blocks include depression, fatigue, burnout, drugs and genetic factors. I provide general suggestions in Chapter 10 for dealing with these.

MYTHS AND MISCONCEPTIONS

Faulty ideas about the creative process can lead to false expectations and unnecessary frustration. This whole book attempts to clear up the major misconceptions, and Chapter 2, in particular, focuses on the worst myths. A few last words about psychological assumptions are now warranted.

Psychologists know that an emotional crisis can be very beneficial. But the common conception is that having a "nervous breakdown" is a very negative thing. In fact, it has a very positive side. As strange as it may sound, a "nervous breakdown" is an opportunity to reorganize one's life in a more positive way, on a more solid foundation. A song by American songwriter Carly Simon says "Don't mind if I fall apart, there's more room in a broken heart." It is a beautiful line that exemplifies what I am referring to. After a relationship breaks up, your life may feel like it's falling apart. You may feel downhearted and distraught. But if you can work through the negative emotions, there's an opportunity for growth and change and a better relationship.

Here's another example specifically regarding the creative process. People who are very compulsive, people who are conformists or authoritarian, tend to dislike ambiguity and disorder. Paul Valerie, a famous poet, said "Disorder is a condition of the mind's fertility. It contains the mind's promise since its fertility depends on the unexpected rather than the expected."

When a person becomes too set in authoritarian attitudes, he tends to demand that things stay the same. He follows tradition too closely and obeys the rules of the book too rigidly. He does not question authority. Now, many people believe this is acceptable behavior. But creativity means questioning what has gone on before and challenging the rules. To be creative, we must often throw out the established order and embrace disorder.

It takes a strong ego and a great deal of inner strength to confront the sacred cows that surround us. A positive self-concept is necessary to stand up for our unique vision and perspective. Without it, our creations will lack originality and will not fulfill our deeper yearning for self-expression.

EXERCISES

★ 1. Assess your environment. Does it support your creativity? Do you have a special place where you create? What are you doing to learn more about the craft or profession in which you want to be creative? Write out a plan for improving your craft.

★ 2. Make a list of fears that block your creativity. Write out a plan for overcoming those fears.

★ 3. Always have paper and pencil ready. If possible, get yourself a hand-held tape recorder. Respect your unconscious creative processes by writing down and/or recording flashes of good ideas. These are gems and pearls—treat them as such.

★ 4. Relaxation can help you recharge your energies when you are exhausted or burned out. It is also the best way to access the subconscious and tap spontaneous, useful insight. Write down three ways you have of relaxing when you are expecting insight.

★ 5. Pick up a newspaper or magazine and study how the writers twist phrases to cleverly get our attention. Do they use a lot of puns? How could you improve on their writing? Take one of your favorite proverbs and convert it into a new headline by giving it a new twist.

★ 6. What are your specific creativity spoilers? Name them. Look at your own conflicts. What have you been avoiding? Are there some thoughts that cause you anxiety when think about them? Is there a conflict in your life that you avoid dealing with? Find the universal story in that conflict and write about it. Give it a title. In fact, it may be very helpful to come up with a title first and then write the story.

★ 7. Focus on change. Take a walk and see the changes in people and in nature. How does it feel to experience these changes?

CHAPTER 6

CLEAN UP YOUR
CREATIVE ECOLOGY

*I can tell you how to get a Nobel Prize . . . have
great teachers.*

**Paul Samuelson,
Nobel laureate economist**

We are all products of our environments. Without a nurturing
environment, our greatest talents can be wasted.

Research shows that many highly creative people grow up in
supportive environments with extremely nurturing parents. These
parents encourage their children to be independent and treat them
as special. They spend a great deal of time, energy and money developing their children's talents and providing tutors or mentors for
them. These parents often work in the same field where their
children will later exhibit great mastery and skill.

Perhaps you are one of the lucky few who grew up in such an
environment. If so, I'll show you how to build on it to maximize your
good fortune. If you are like most of us, however, you struggle to
create a supportive environment for your work. As part of your creativity enhancement program, you must first evaluate how your
present environment adds to or takes away from your creative
energies. Your creative environment includes not only your physical

83

space, but your social and economic surroundings as well. Ecology comes from the Greek word, *oikos,* meaning *house.* So, cleaning up your creative ecology means getting your house in order!

Organizing your life so you can release your creative energies and realize your dreams is part of this process. You must set goals and then structure your life in order to accomplish these goals. Sometimes this means making great sacrifices or doing things just a little bit different than the next guy. You might have to postpone a vacation or forgo a highly desired pleasure in order to finish your project. You may need to make some tough decisions that will affect your career or change your lifestyle. A decision to pursue additional schooling or a careful analysis of how to expand your business can mean the difference between success and failure.

And don't think that great creators take these matters lightly. While he was working on his theory of evolution, Darwin was wrestling with his decision to get married. In his notebooks, he wrote: "If not marry, TRAVEL? Europe—yes? America????? If marry— means limited—Feel duty to work for money. London life, nothing but Society, no country, no tours, no large Zoolog; collect., no books."

Clearly, Darwin did not want his creative energies taken up with the superficialities of London society or the need to earn money. On the other hand, he weighed the benefits of marriage and children. "Children—(if it please God)—constant companion (friend in old age) who will feel interested in one, object to be beloved and played with . . . Forced to visit and receive relations *but terrible loss of time*" (Barlow, 1958).

Creating an ecological system that nurtures your creativity is an ongoing process. It never ends. You will need to make constant adjustments to keep it in a balanced state. Your creativity environment is a dynamic interplay of numerous subsystems, including physical, social and economic spheres. Looking at each subsystem in greater detail is a first step in cleaning up your creative ecology.

PHYSICAL ENVIRONMENT

I recommend that you have a physical space you can call your Creativity Center. This doesn't mean it will be the *only* place where you create, but it serves as a home base for your creative work. It is a place where you can go to replenish and recharge your creative energies.

Executives have their offices. Artists have their studios. Carpenters have their workshops. Create a place for yourself. Put your tools on a desk or work table. Make sure you have plenty of supplies such as pencils, tape recorders, clay, hammers and screw drivers, or paper and brushes so you can work whenever you feel like it. This workplace could be in the garage, in the den, or even in a corner of a bedroom. Wherever it is, fill it with items that inspire you to create.

Put up a picture of a creative person you greatly admire. Display an object you have created and you are particularly proud of. These items are deeply associated within your mind with positive creative activity on your part. Having them in front of you elicits creative behaviors.

Remember Pavlov's dog? After repeatedly hearing a bell ring just before he got fed, he began to salivate at the sound of the bell. He associated the bell with the food. You will see in Chapter 8 that this is called *anchoring*. Like Pavlov's dog, we are creatures of habit and subject to this kind of conditioning. We will be more likely to engage in creative acts when we surround ourselves with stimuli that have been associated with creative behavior.

We are also subject to the process called *imitation learning*. We imitate behavior that is being rewarded. Successful creative people serve as good imitation models.

Your workplace is your retreat. We are bombarded daily with constant demands for our attention. Our energies are usually focused on everyday tasks unrelated to our cherished creativity dreams. Your workplace must be a spot where you can regroup and refocus yourself. Sit and do nothing, or meditate to help you relax. Center yourself and clear the cobwebs from your mind. Do whatever it takes to listen to your inner voice and commit yourself to what's truly important to you.

We must reserve a little back-shop, all our own, entirely free, wherein to establish our true liberty and principal retreat and solitude.

Montaigne, French philosopher

Financier Wayne Silby, founder of the Calvert Group of money funds, uses a sensory deprivation tank to get away from the distractions of everyday life. He floats in warm water, sealed off from light and sound. In this environment, he discovers innovative investment ideas.

One of my clients, Isabel, couldn't expand her business because she was without office space. Her cash flow was too small to justify renting. Her business was floundering with disorganization and she was overwhelmed by confusion. She decided to make space in her garage. With room to organize herself and take refuge from her family, she could now concentrate and think clearly about her business. She developed a clear business plan, and within months she doubled her cash flow.

Your work space must be a place where you feel free to experiment. It's your secret hideaway where you can make a mess or organize your work, whatever you want. In this space, you are free to make mistakes, to let your hair hang down and contact "the muse."

Your workplace must not become a prison, however. Whenever you feel you are going stale, think about changing environments. When Picasso was trying to work out some new perspectives in his art and sculpture, he changed his studio. When he was struggling with his studies of the great painter, Velasquez, he apparently abandoned his studio in the drawing room and, in the words of Pierre Daix in *Picasso, Life and Art,* established "a new studio in the attic, previously left to the pigeons. Here he would grapple in solitude with Velasquez for over four months . . . without interruption . . . which fits his usual pattern of attempting to master a new environment."

Dr. Jean Landy helped Brian Wilson of the Beach Boys break through his old blocks by changing his ecosystem. Brian had been creatively dry for a long time. Dr. Landy first took him off drugs. He said he had to bring Brian Wilson back physically. Besides exercise, medication, vitamins and diet, he also changed "the physical environment because he was living in a dark room with no windows."

Another of my clients, Mike, had established an area where he could write every morning. But when he felt like he was getting into a rut, he changed environments. He wrote at the beach or at a quiet Italian restaurant where he would have lunch and work for hours. In this atmosphere, he felt like he was indulging himself and "being artsy." It satisfied his romantic image of Bohemian writers and it worked. In this new environment, Mike not only produced more interesting stories, but his Italian improved!

Jeff, on the other hand, put up a picture of Einstein in his real estate office. The picture of this great scientist inspires him to use his imagination to come up with novel solutions. Sometimes Jeff sits in his office and does nothing. Slowly, looking at the picture and his books on the shelf, he gets inspired. Within minutes, he is busy on the phone or writing up new advertising copy for his clients. He says, "Sometimes I feel down and discouraged when I first walk in the office. I then take a deep breath and let things happen. I don't pressure myself. Usually my mind wanders and I will eventually recall something I had been thinking about earlier that day or, sometimes, days before. Then, suddenly, I feel a surge of energy. I recapture that old enthusiasm that makes this job fun."

SOCIAL ENVIRONMENT

Creativity is perhaps best acquired through association with creativity.

Cattell and Butcher,
Creativity researchers

Your social environment consists of all the people who surround you on a regular basis. These include family, friends, mentors, allies, enemies, competitors and what I call "psychic vampires." Do these people add to or deplete your creative energies?

Family

The family in which you are reared plays a significant role in shaping your creativity. After the womb, it is the first environment to shape our personality. Through our interaction with family members we learn about the world and ourselves. Our curiosity and willingness to take risks are greatly influenced by those early experiences. Our sense of competence and self-esteem are formed by the type of support that we receive while growing up. In addition, we are affected by such non-obvious factors as birth order and family size.

Miller and Gerard (1979) studied family influences on the development of children's creativity and confirmed what other researchers had found. Your birth position in the family (first, middle or last) influences later creativity. For example, later children may be more inclined to go into the arts than firstborns.

Researchers have found that parents of highly creative children treat them as someone special. These parents also set a positive example and encourage creative behaviors by being open and creative themselves. They are not so concerned with what others think and are less rigid about following rules.

But what does that have to do with your present social situation and creative behavior?

Whether or not you currently live with your parents, you are most likely still influenced by them. One conclusion I have drawn from the research and my clinical experience is that family-of-origin influences are ongoing and can have a powerful impact on behavior. You need to assess your situation to determine whether you are being nurtured in your creative efforts. After an honest analysis, if your family is undermining your efforts, you need to take action.

Sometimes professional help may be needed. Often, however, all you really need is an honest self-appraisal and a decision to modify your patterns of behavior. Honoring and encouraging creativity in family members is perhaps the best way to increase the probability of support from them.

What about your other family? That is, your own children and significant other. How is this environment currently structured? Are you contemplating changes, like relocating or having more children? These and other family decisions will affect your creativity.

Studies show that the number of children you have affects your creativity. The greater the number of children, the less the creativity outside the home. Parents with large families tend to be creative in the home and family rather than in outside projects. It takes a lot of energy to raise a large family and there is usually not much left over for work outside the family. Of course, there are exceptions. Many large families appear to be highly creative because of the energy generated from friendly sibling rivalry and the efficiency that comes from working together constantly.

Regardless of what we may conclude about the exact role of the family, you will have to take this aspect of your social environment into account. Ask yourself the following questions:

1. How is my family affecting and being affected by my projects?

2. Does my family nurture my creativity? Am I nurturing of my family's creativity?

3. Can I get away from my family when I need to?

4. What type of example am I setting for my children?

5. Do I let my family participate in my projects? Do they share in the joys and triumphs of my accomplishments? Or do they share only in the sorrows and defeats?

Friends and Allies

. . . alignment means that people agree on what their purpose is and specifically what they want to become over the course of a number of years. Without alignment we work at cross-purposes.

William C. Miller

We could ask many of the above questions about our friends, collaborators, mentors and allies. Today's world makes it increasingly evident that creativity is a social endeavor. There is very little that we accomplish that does not involve the efforts of other people, from two-person collaborations to the workings of multinational corporations. Projects that involve expensive technology need the capital available in large corporations. For example, it takes millions of dollars to make a movie. The resources of a large hospital are necessary to do medical research as well as to perform innovative surgery.

In addition to the technical and financial resources these networks of collaborators offer, they provide us with contacts. It is still very true that "it's not what you know, but who you know." To get a key position in an industry you love, to get signed as an artist in the entertainment industry, or to get good sales leads, it's important to have "friends in high places" or at least in the right places. I'm not recommending that you sell out or compromise your cherished values to get ahead. I am saying that you need to consider the importance of networking for success in today's world.

Assess the industry you are in or aspire to be in. Ask yourself:

1. How far do I want to go?

2. What are my criteria for success and what price am I willing to pay for it?

3. How many contacts do I already have in this field?

4. Where can I meet more people I can network with?

5. What organizations or groups of people with similar interests can I join?

> *The important thing is to get people involved, to participate and contribute.*
>
> **Tom, political stategist and
> former executive for a Fortune 100
> conglomerate**

Dean Simonton, professor of psychology at the University of California and author of Greatness, reports that most Nobel prize winners had past Nobel prize winners as mentors, or at least sur-rounded themselves with highly creative people in their field. He also claims that scientists "in networks with other scientific creators have longer and more productive careers than those who are isolated." The lesson: Surround yourself with other people who are actively engaged in creating similar works and who stimulate your creativity. Don't be afraid to collaborate.

Other Allies

Other allies include teachers, agents, promoters, managers and anyone who respects and supports your goals and dreams. They help you when you need them most. When they make business deals with you, they are fair and look out for *your* interests as well as theirs.

Look for business relationships that emphasize cooperation over competition. This is easier said than done, however. You'd be surprised how many people hold to the philosophy of "every man for himself." They treat friendships and even intimate relationships like a win-lose game. They have difficulty conceiving of win-win relationships or transactions. This is particularly problematic when it goes unrecognized. Know who you are dealing with *before you make a deal.*

I learned this lesson the hard way. In the early 1980s I was negotiating a partnership agreement with two colleagues. During the difficult task of dividing up each partner's rights and responsibil-ities, we reflected on the agreement-making process. The partner to my left, a psychiatrist, said "I see this as a friendly poker game." The partner to my right, who was into competitive sports, said, "I see it more like a tennis match." I told them that I didn't see it as a com-petitive game at all. To me, it was like having a piece of pie in front of us and trying to figure out the fairest and most equitable way to divide it up.

They saw our partnership as a win-lose game rather than a win-win situation. I should have known then the serious trouble that lay ahead for our partnership.

Enemies and Competitors

"Stay close to your friends and keep your enemies even closer." This old proverb underlines the need to know who your enemies are and what they are doing. In an ideal world, we would not have enemies. But realistically, we must acknowledge that we can't please everybody and we may displease some people immensely. It is also true that the bigger the project the more people involved in the work, the greater the chance for disagreements and potential enemies. This is especially true where fame and fortune are at stake.

My recommendation is to always be fair. If you are in a situation where you get the better of a deal, don't gloat. Don't pour salt on wounds unless you want to fuel the fires of anger and hatred.

Our enemies and competitors occasionally bring out our worst emotions: anger, envy and jealousy. I've seen clients spend enormous amounts of time and energy brooding over real or imagined betrayals, slights or other interpersonal conflicts. Usually these are feelings coupled with a desire for revenge.

Negative feelings restrict, constrict and isolate you. They zap the flow of your creative energies. When we invest our mental and emotional energy in "the enemy," we waste our precious resources. Obsessions of these types also fuel the negative conflict. It becomes a vicious circle—the more you obsess, the greater the conflict becomes.

If you find yourself filled with negative emotions, first use the relaxation and programming methods described in Chapter 7. This will help you refocus. Then look deeply within to uncover the source of your anger, envy and jealousy. Don't be a victim. Don't take it personally, and don't bang your head against the wall. Detach yourself from the emotions and look at the conflict objectively. In other words, see it as a challenge in which to use your creative problem-solving skills. We'll come back to this in Chapter 11 where we'll learn to cultivate a higher state of mind. But for now, remember that success is the best revenge!

Psychic Vampires

Psychic vampires are creativity killers. At the very least, they waste your precious time. In the worst cases, they can destroy your life. You need to watch out for them because they are sometimes difficult to detect.

The narcissistic personality discussed in Chapter 4 is an example of the psychic vampire. He is charming and intelligent. He will use you for his purposes and discard you when you are no longer useful. He will lead you astray and suck your energy with promises of pots of gold. "Stick with me, Kid" seems to be his lure. He holds out the carrot on a stick and manipulates you into investing time, energy and money in his projects. "This is the big breakthrough we've been waiting for," he tells you.

Psychic vampires are often highly successful and creative people themselves. Picasso is said to have wrecked several lives in his path. More than one of those closest to him committed suicide.

Why are we attracted to Psychic vampires? I've come to the conclusion that the problem lies in our own weaknesses or unfulfilled aspects of our personalities. For example, if we are too conservative and controlled, we are charmed by the apparent spontaneity of narcissists. They appear free and uninhibited where we feel self-conscious and dull. They are charming when we are boring. We envy their daring and their ability to speak their minds. We must recognize our weakness for psychic vampires and protect ourselves from them. We need to clean up our creative environment by learning to detect them. If we don't, we are in for many heartbreaks and loss of creative opportunities.

Here are a few suggestions for coping with narcissists:

1. Keep some emotional distance.

2. Don't get sucked into trying to change them or into thinking they will change when they've had enough.

3. Be careful not to insult them. Unless you really want a revengeful enemy waiting for the chance to get even.

4. Don't let them walk all over you. Don't feel guilty when you interrupt them or assert yourself. You'll only feel worse about your own passivity and the shame will be a downer.

Narcissists take kindness for weakness, and they prey on weakness. They may be sadistic and blame you if you allow them to victimize you. Don't play the victim. See them as users and protect yourself.

Guilt Manipulators and Dependents

Although they are the most dramatic and seductive creativity killers, psychic vampires aren't the only enemies. Equally problematic are people who manipulate your guilt and sense of responsibility. Guilt manipulators feel threatened by your need for creative freedom. They may be dependent on you and fear being abandoned. Their need for you may make you feel needed, but you may pay a high price for this sense of security. Don't reward their dependent behavior. Don't allow yourself to be manipulated by guilt. Learn to assert yourself. Help them become independent. Assert your right to pursue your life as you wish. Assert your right to be irresponsible and have some fun once in a while. Encourage them to do the same.

ECONOMIC ENVIRONMENT

No matter what, money is always a big part of life. It's the context within which we make decisions. It determines how large a workplace you can afford, the quantity and quality of tools you have to work with, and the resources you have at your disposal to manufacture and market your product. It affects how much time and energy you have available to devote to your dreams.

Cecilia is typical of many of my workshop participants. She is frustrated because she cannot devote her entire life to doing what she loves most. She is a clothing designer and hates having to get a job outside the clothing design world. Many of my clients also would like to devote their entire lives to their chosen creative work. They are unhappy because they have to take day jobs while they get their act together. They dream that someday they will not have to worry about money and will be able to devote all their time and energies to doing only what they love to do . . . without compromise.

This is definitely a real source of frustration for many people. But how realistic is the dream of financial freedom or of doing only what we love? Often we have an infantile wish to have everything we want. It reflects a desire to be omnipotent and loved unconditionally. At times, this can serve as an excuse, a way of diverting energy from the more difficult task we face—creating an environment where we can satisfy our economic needs and still enjoy working at what we love. This need is often an excuse for nonaction and is supported by statements such as "If only . . . ."

The reality is that our concern for money and our need for more of it never ends. The movie producer with a million-dollar budget can always complain that he could do so much more with five million dollars. After we get the large office in Beverly Hills, imagine what we could do with another office on the beach or with several assistants to run our errands while we come up with innovative and exciting ideas!

Given that your relationship with money will most likely be a continual juggling act, what can you do? There are probably at least several options that are available to you. You could:

1. Marry someone rich.

2. Find a sponsor.

3. Take a job in a position related to your chosen field. If you want to be a writer, work for a publisher or be a copyreader for a magazine or newspaper.

4. Do volunteer work or an internship in your field of interest. This may not help your money problems immediately, but over time it could lead to working and earning money in that field.

5. Start a business using your own services and products. Along these lines, you can consult the Small Business Administration for advice. Retired businessmen may be able to help you write a business plan or find a partner or venture capital.

6. Make a budget of your essential needs. Learn to live on less until you can get your career going.

7. Read up on money management. Take a seminar or listen to the audio cassette/workshop course by Joseph Dominquez, *Transforming your Relationship with Money*. It's available

through the New Road Map Foundation in Seattle, Washington.

To evaluate your relationship to money:

1. List four sayings you have about money. For example:

    (a) A penny saved is a penny earned.
    (b) Penny wise and pound foolish.

2. Play a word-association game. Very quickly, list ten words that you associate with money.

3. How would your creative work change if you had twice as much money as you have today? Three times as much?

4. Pretend you don't need to work for money. Describe your typical work day. Be specific and detailed.

Your ecosystem is made up of more than the subsystems I have just described. but this will get you started. The important thing to remember is that we are greatly affected by our surroundings. We do not live in a vacuum. Create an environment of friends and allies that will share your joys and triumphs. It's great to go at it alone, but dreams shared and missions accomplished with others can be twice as sweet.

EXERCISES

1. Assess your Creativity Center. How often do you go there? Can you be alone there for long periods of time? Do you feel free to make mistakes or make a mess there? Are your tools handy? Is it a special place, a refuge?

2. Take your tools and try out a new work environment. Make it a fun place like the beach or an artsy restaurant or bookstore. Perhaps somewhere in the woods would be more inspirational for you. Go where you feel free and alive.

3. Examine your feelings of envy and jealousy. How much time did you spend this week thinking about a wrong that was done to you or a tense interpersonal conflict? Did you brood or did you problem-solve?

4. We often tie up a lot of energy in anger and negative emotions. Is there anyone in your past that you need to forgive? Let go and recoup that lost energy.

5 Do you need to develop assertiveness skills? Read a book on assertiveness training. Learn what your rights are. Practice saying no. Write down the names of those people in your life that do not respect your creativity space. In what ways are they "psychic vampires?"

6. Make a list of your top supporters and allies. How have they helped you move toward your goals? Reciprocate by doing something for them. Think deeply into their needs. What is their creativity domain? What are their dreams and aspirations? Help them achieve their goals.

7. Identify the top people in your geographical area with whom you can either collaborate or to whom you can become an apprentice. Start a collaborative relationship. If you're not ready for this step, look for a mentor in your chosen field.

8. Where does your money go? Make a budget. Decide how you could cut down on your expenses. How much life energy are you sacrificing to obtain material things you could do without? If you did without these material items, how much more money would you have? And then, how much more time would you have to devote to your most valued projects?

9. Is the climate of your business or organization conducive to creativity? Are employees encouraged to come up with new ideas or solutions? Are there special sessions for brainstorming? Is innovation rewarded?

✔ 10. Assess your needs for support staff. Do you need a manager, booking agent, sales rep, project consultant or an assistant? Are there free support services you can tap into such as the Small Business Administration or the National Association for the Self-Employed?

✔ 11. Review Appendix 2 for resources that might help you in your work.

PART THREE

_____

Digging In: Easy-To-Use Tools of The Quest

Satisfaction of one's curiosity is one of the greatest sources of happiness in life.

Linus Pauling

CHAPTER 7

SELF-HYPNOSIS AND AFFIRMATIONS

Hypnosis is a way of making a reality. If you know that something you want will happen in a specific reality, then use that reality to create what you want. If it doesn't happen in any reality that you know of, then create a reality in which it would happen.

John Grinder and Richard Bandler,
Trance-formations

What we believe in greatly determines what will come true. A medicine man tells a perfectly healthy tribesman that he will die within 24 hours. If he believes in the magical powers of the medicine man, the tribesman will die within 24 hours. Most likely, he will become extremely disturbed and die of cardiac arrest.

A hypnotized person is told that a blister will form on her finger when the hypnotist touches it with a lit cigarette. The hypnotist touches her with the rubber end of a lead pencil and the hypnotized person develops a blister. Why? Because she *believes* she is being touched with a lit cigarette.

There are many cases of trauma patients who have walked in spite of being told by their medical doctors that they would never walk again. These patients walked because they would not accept the doctor's prognosis. Were these miracles or just strong beliefs? Or are miracles the products of strong beliefs against overwhelming odds?

In some cases of terminal cancer, patients were told that only a miracle would save their lives. The patients and their families believed in miracles. The patients survived, again, against overwhelming odds.

A group of children are tested and their IQs are about average. The researchers want to find out what effect, if any, teachers' expectations have on student IQs. They tell a schoolteacher that the children in her classroom are exceptionally bright. Within a few months, the same children are retested. Lo and behold! Their IQ scores are now higher than they were before and higher than the scores of a control group of children. What happened? The researchers concluded that, because the teacher *believed* the children were exceptionally bright, she treated them special and they performed as such.

Isn't that interesting? Not only do our beliefs about ourselves affect our behavior, but so do other people's beliefs about us. Why? Simple. Because we internalize what other people believe about us. We take what they believe about us and make these our own beliefs about ourselves.

If this is so, then shouldn't we be examining our belief systems? You bet. Which of the following beliefs do you hold about yourself?

1. You are not the creative type.

2. If you try to be different, people will think you are a snob.

3. You're crazy to think you can be a writer.

4. You're too old to really start doing something new and original.

5. You don't deserve to be happy and fulfilled.

6. You're not special enough to stand out.

7. You don't have the right to expect people to support your creative dreams.

8. You're selfish to indulge in your dreams.

The following sentence-completion game is a good way to tap into your belief system.

Finish the following sentences:

1. I think money is . . .

2. I could do great things if . . .

3. The key to success is . . .

4. I think famous people are . . .

5. Being older means . . .

6. I believe magic is . . .

PAST PROGRAMMING

Our beliefs are, in part, the result of our old programming. Most are childhood messages implanted in our brains when we were very open to suggestion. These beliefs became deeply imbedded because they occurred during periods of high emotionality and susceptibility. Usually, they were repeated constantly.

Children are sponges. As children, we are totally open to the world. What we take in filters into the deepest recesses of our minds. And what we were told by our parents and teachers had profound effects on us.

We were being programmed even before we learned to speak, however. We learned through images, nonverbal messages and modeling. Images of parents scolding us helped to form our concept of whether we were good or bad, and what was acceptable or unacceptable behavior. Because they were formed by a nonverbal process, these messages are now less accessible to the conscious mind.

Hopefully, most of the messages we received during those early years were positive ones. But how do we change the negative, unwanted messages that are holding us back? How do we delete or modify the messages that are sabotaging our creative projects? How do we rid ourselves of this old programming?

The answer lies in creating not only new words for ourselves but also new images. We must then filter these images down to the deeper recesses of our minds. If possible, we must embed them into the tissues, the muscles, the bones and the very marrow of our being.

How do we create these images?

NEW PROGRAMMING

When you already have a belief, there's no room for a new one unless you weaken the old belief first.
Richard Bandler

In order to reprogram ourselves and change those deeply embedded messages, we must recreate the childlike mind. We must regain an openness to the world, the vulnerability and the innocent acceptance of new images, feelings and perceptions. However, we want to do this in a controlled environment so we know that the images we are creating for ourselves are positive images. In a sense, it's a regression to an infantile stage but regression in the service of the adult mind, or what Freud called regression in the service of the ego. That is, we are regressing in a controlled way and bringing consciousness and unconsciousness together.

HYPNOSIS: A BRIEF HISTORY

Hypnosis is a powerful method I have used for reprogramming and changing beliefs. I teach my clients self-hypnosis so they can reprogram themselves in the privacy of their own homes.

My booklet, *Self Hypnosis Made Simple*, outlines the history of hypnosis and some myths associated with it. Hypnosis has come a long way since the days of its founders, Mesmer and Braid. Mesmer used to "mesmerize" his subjects by using magnets to influence their electrical fields. Braid took the word *hypnos* from the Greek word for sleep and emphasized the importance of suggestion in hypnosis. Freud used hypnosis early in his career. He declared that if psychotherapy was ever to become widely accepted, hypnosis would certainly be useful for rapid results.

More recently, Milton Erikson's work has placed hypnosis on solid scientific footing. His creative work with hypnosis is well documented by two of his students, Ernest Rossi and Margaret Ryan in their four volume set *The Seminars, Workshops, and Lectures of Milton H. Erickson.*

The American Psychological Association published the *Handbook of Clinical Hypnosis* in 1993. The handbook contains current scientific knowledge about hypnosis and its use in treating a multitude of symptoms and in changing behavior. Hypnosis has now become a very legitimate and respectable tool used by today's psychologists.

Bandler and Grinder have modernized the practice of hypnosis with their method of Neuro Linguistic Programming. They explain how we are constantly being "hypnotized" in everyday conversation and how we program ourselves through the use of language. If you are interested in learning more about their techniques, read *Frogs into Princes or Trance-formations.* These are good introductory books that are full of examples about how we hypnotize ourselves and others in everyday communication.

WHAT IS HYPNOSIS?

Hypnosis itself, as far as I'm concerned, is simply using yourself as a biofeedback mechanism.
John Grinder and Richard Bandler

Simply stated, hypnosis is a method or technique whereby suggestions or instructions are placed in the mind while the critical and judgmental faculties are temporarily suspended.

Normally we are guarded, cautious and skeptical about information that is coming to us. We filter information coming to us through our censors. That is why it is very difficult to access the deeper layers of our minds. But that is exactly what we must do to help us produce deep and profound changes in our personalities.

Imagine that the mind is like the ocean and our conscious mind is like the surface of the ocean. When we normally interact with the world, we are only swimming on the surface of the water. In order to really understand our minds, we must go into the very deep layers below the surface. As explorers of the subconscious, we begin to imagine ourselves as divers into these deeper levels.

The surface level is very turbulent, tense and noisy. Sometimes we arrive at areas of turbulence underneath the surface because, like the ocean, there are rivers running underneath. As we go into deeper levels, we begin to experience calmer waters. As you learn more about hypnosis, you access ever deeper layers of your mind and learn how to make profound changes in your personality.

Likewise, during the normal course of the day, we are bombarded with sounds, sights, smells, etc. Our senses are constantly exposed to stimulation that we try to organize and understand. In order to do this, we stay on the surface and focus on the demands of the external world.

We therefore use our critical faculties to organize the incoming information. We have learned from our past mistakes to be cautious and to see only those things that are not too painful or that do not violate our preconceived notions.

Hypnotizing Yourself

One way to achieve hypnosis is to first get into a state of relaxation. This state of relaxation can be brought about by any method you have at your disposal. It can be as simple as sitting in a quiet place and taking a few slow, deep breaths. If you are in a quiet place and not involved in any activity that requires your attention, you could do this right now. Don't do it if you must pay attention to what you are doing. For example, don't do this while driving.

Since our eyes are sense organs that take in a lot of information for processing, it might help to close your eyes and eliminate the external sources of distraction. Close your eyes, then, and take three slow, deep breaths.

Are you relaxed? If so, you are now entering into the beginning stage of a hypnotic trance. If not, here are a few of the conditions that facilitate the entrance into the hypnotic state:

1. Relaxation.

2. Either passivity of mind or focused attention.

3. Removal of as many sources of outside stimulation as possible.

4. An expectation that you will enter into a hypnotic state.

Here are conditions that impede the entrance into the hypnotic state:

1. Trying too hard (although a good hypnotist can use this to make going into trance easier).

2. A skeptical, overly critical or analytical attitude.

3. Doubt that you can enter into a hypnotic state.

The next thing to do while in this state of relaxation is to give yourself a positive suggestion. For example, while in this state of easy relaxation, say to yourself, "I am feeling more self-confident with every day that goes by." Say this to yourself very slowly. Now say it nine times in a row. As you say it, picture yourself the way you would like to be. That is, see yourself in your mind's eye (your imagination) as a person who is happy with himself or herself, is very self-confident and feels really good. Take a few minutes to visualize this.

Congratulations! You have just hypnotized yourself and given yourself a powerful autosuggestion. You have now experienced what it is like to be hypnotized. Next, you will learn more about how to achieve a deeper state of relaxation and how to give yourself more complex and more powerful suggestions.

Many people do not know that they have been hypnotized because they have false expectations about what the trance state feels like. They may have heard that they will be asleep or that they will be unconscious. They may also think they will act like zombies or be in a stupor. Here are some descriptions of the light hypnotic state:

1. Arms and/or legs feel like they are floating.

2. Arms and/or legs may feel heavy.

3. Eyelids may feel heavy, may tremble or flutter.

4. Fingers or other parts of the body may twitch.

5. Facial muscles feel relaxed and the lower jaw may fall sightly, with the lips becoming slightly parted.

6. Feelings like just before going to sleep.

7. Seeing things as if one is dreaming.

As you become more proficient, you will be able to enter into a deeper trance if you chose. What you have achieved at this point is a state of light hypnosis. To arrive at medium trance and even deep trance, all you need is practice. Additional instruction in this chapter will give you more powerful tools to make your practice more fruitful.

Awakening

What if you can't awaken from your hypnotic state? This is a fear that some people have when they began hypnosis. Be assured that no one has ever remained in a hypnotic trance forever. On the other hand, you may enjoy the state of relaxation brought about by hypnosis so much that you won't want to come out of it for a while. Usually, you'll come out of it anyway after a few minutes.

The worse that can happen is that you will fall asleep and awaken later in your normal state. If you wish, you can say the following statement at the beginning of your session to control how long you will be in a state of trance: "I will wake up to my normal state within 30 minutes [or whatever time you allow] of starting my session." If you wish, you may also set an alarm clock and say to yourself that you will wake up to your normal consciousness when the alarm rings. Finally, you can say, "If there is any emergency, I will awaken immediately and I will be alert and normal in every way." However, my clinical experience has shown that this is really not necessary. You will soon realize how much control you have in awakening when you want to. Also, as you learn more about how to "program" yourself, you will learn how to ensure that you will come out of your trance at precisely the moment you desire.

More Powerful Suggestions

. . . change happens constantly, and easily, and making it work for you is a matter of understanding how to run your own brain.
Richard Bandler

Now you will learn to achieve a deeper state of relaxation. The deeper the relaxation, the deeper the new messages will go into your mind. I've included the following script to be used for deep relaxation. For best results, record it in a very slow, relaxing manner into a tape recorder. Then place yourself in a quiet setting and listen to your recording.

If you are interested in my recording of this text or any of my hypnosis tapes, use the order form in the back of the book.

Relaxation Script

"Hello. The following instructions are a guide to help you attain a state of deep relaxation. If you follow the suggestions, you will achieve a pleasurable and enjoyable feeling of easy relaxation. First, start out by finding a comfortable position where you can listen to my voice and let yourself relax. You may either sit or lie down, whichever is more comfortable for you. Let your arms rest loosely beside you. Close your eyes and fix your gaze upwards on a point between your eyes, about the middle of your forehead. Now take three slow, deep breaths . . . Breathe in slowly . . . (pause) . . . With each exhalation, let yourself go into a deeper state of relaxation . . . (pause) . . . good. Take three deep breaths. That's it. Now, as you begin to breathe easily and more freely, let yourself drift into a deeper level of relaxation . . . .

Now that you are breathing easily and drifting into deeper levels of relaxation, you can relax even more by letting all your muscles go loose and limp. Focus your attention on the soles of your feet and let all your muscles become like loose rubber bands. That's it. As the muscles relax, the blood circulates more easily and you can feel a certain warmth coming over your feet. Imagine your feet being soaked in warm water. Let yourself experience those warm, plea-surable sensations . . . good . . . . When you have felt your feet getting warmer, let that feeling of warmth and relaxation travel up your body . . . up into your ankle . . . your calves . . . and up past your knees and into your thighs. As the feeling of warmth passes through those areas, let your muscles become loose and limp. As you let go and release your muscles, you allow the blood to circulate more freely and the feeling of warm relaxation increases.

Be-Here-Now
(Begin to slow down. Draw out the words.)

Continue relaxing as you allow those warm, pleasurable feelings of relaxation to travel up to your stomach . . . . Now your entire body, from the tips of your toes to your stomach, is enveloped in these comfortable, enjoyable feelings of relaxation. All those muscles are becoming loose and relaxed. Let these feelings continue upwards to your diaphragm or solar plexus. This is the area just above your navel and below your ribs. It is known as the center of nervous energies. As you relax this area and let your breath enter into the center, you will experience a calmness and peacefulness entering into your entire body. As your body continues to relax, let your mind do the same. Let your mind drift into a calm and peaceful feeling of relaxation . . . good . . . . Just continue enjoying these feelings and continue going down and down into a deeper state of relaxation . . . .

When you begin to experience this increased calmness and peace of mind, let that peacefulness and calmness spread into your heart and over your entire chest . . . that's it. Let all the muscles of your chest become loose and limp. As you let go of these muscles, all those tensions begin to leave your chest and your breathing becomes easier and easier. Feel that greater openness inside your chest cavity. Just let your breathing become slow and easy.

Be-Here-Now

Now focus your attention on your hands and arms. Imagine your hand becoming warmer and warmer and let that feeling of warmth travel up from your fingertips . . . to the palms of your hands . . . to your wrists . . . your forearms and going all the way up to your shoulders . . . . As the warmth travels upwards, let your muscles become loose and limp and relaxed. Now let the feeling of relaxation travel downward from your shoulders, down on both sides of your spine and down your spinal column. Let all those muscles become loose and limp and feel those pleasurable sensations going downward over your entire body . . . down into you lower back . . . continuing downward into your buttocks . . . to the back of your thighs, down to the back of your calves and down into the heels of your feet. When that feeling of relaxation reaches the heels of your feet, let it travel across your soles to your toes and upward again over your legs, into your stomach and chest again.

Be-Here-Now

Just take a few seconds to enjoy this feeling of deep relaxation. That's it . . . . Now if you will focus your attention on the back of your neck, you can increase your feeling of relaxation. Let those muscles become loose and limp. Let all those tensions in your neck just melt away. As your neck relaxes, you will feel your breathing become easier. Let the feeling of relaxation flow easily up to the top of your head. When it reaches the top of your head, let it radiate outward, relaxing every tiny muscle and nerve of your scalp. Let it flow downwards into your forehead and around your eyebrows. As the relaxation radiates over your eyes, feel those tiny muscles and nerves around your eyes becoming heavier and heavier. Become totally and utterly relaxed.

The feeling of relaxation continues into every muscle of your face as you drift into deeper and deeper levels of relaxation. The feeling of relaxation flows into the muscles around your lips, into your cheeks and behind your ears . . . into the muscles of your jaw. As the muscles of your jaw relax, you feel your lips part slightly. As your jaw drops, the feeling of relaxation increases and radiates to your entire head and down to your toes . . . (pause) . . . Now you continue relaxing with each breath. As the breath enters your nostrils, let your attention focus inwardly into deeper levels of your innermost self. Following your breath, you feel yourself relaxing deep within your heart . . . into your internal organs . . . down . . .

down, into your stomach and down into your intestines. Down to the marrow of your bones, you feel yourself becoming more and more totally relaxed.

You are now bathed in the wonderful feeling of deep relaxation. At first with this tape and later without it, you will be able to relax more deeply, more easily and more quickly with each succeeding session. You will find yourself becoming more relaxed in your daily life as these feelings of relaxation transfer over to your daily activities. Practice this relaxation at least once a day. As you practice, you will become more and more familiar with the feeling of relaxation, inner peacefulness, inner tranquility and inner calmness. The more familiar you are with this place, the easier it will be to get here.

This is a place where you can . . . feel wonderful . . . feel recharged . . . your body is totally relaxed . . . your mind is totally relaxed but extremely alert. You feel totally in the present moment. Totally at one with yourself.

When you feel you have reached a deep level of relaxation and have become familiar with this feeling, you may begin to shorten the script. Use the phrases that help you to relax . . . eventually use one word that symbolizes, for you, this feeling of deep relaxation. It can be any word such as relax or let go. Chose a word that serves as a signal for you to return to this deep state of relaxation. However, it is preferable to make it a word only you will know so you will be in complete control of when you get to this state. While in this state, repeat that word several times, associating it with the feeling you are in now. By associating the word you have chosen with the feeling of relaxation, you will condition yourself so the word itself will evoke the experience of total relaxation. Remember, choose a word and repeat it often while experiencing this feeling of deep relaxation.

If you wish to remain in this relaxed state or go to sleep, you may awaken yourself now just enough to do whatever is necessary to turn off the tape recorder and return to this deep state of rest. Later, when you want to, you will awaken, feeling fully awake, alert and full of pep and energy.

If you wish to return to your normal state, I am going to count from one to five and you will return to your normal consciousness.

You will be refreshed and alert. One . . . experience this deep state of relaxation for one last time at this session, remembering all the feelings, thoughts and sensations you feel so that you can return easily and quickly on your next session. Two . . . you begin to leave this place, still maintaining a feeling of relaxation, but becoming more alert and awake. Three . . . all the muscles of your body feel alive and full of energy. Your entire body feels like it is bathed in cool, fresh, spring water. Energy, pep and vitality are entering into all the tiny muscles and nerves of your body. Four. You are aware of all the sounds and smells of this room. All your five senses are totally awake and normal. You are feeling full of pep and energy, charged and ready to awaken. Your face feels fresh and bathed in cool spring water. Five . . . fully awake . . . (say this with energy) . . . Open your eyes, take a deep breath, stretch and feel fully awake!

EVERYDAY HYPNOSIS

Now that you've learned what hypnosis is, we can begin to identify how it's used every day. Hypnosis is used in every type of relationship where influence and persuasion are the goals. It is also used when we want to establish a close bond of communication.

Persuasion is the purpose of advertising. Advertising distracts us momentarily by an image, such as a sexy woman, a fast car or appetizing food. The image will distract our critical, judgmental mind. While our critical mind is momentarily distracted, an idea is programmed into the deeper levels of our more open, vulnerable, naive consciousness. That is why going to sleep in front of the television set should be avoided. As we go to sleep, we are very vulnerable and open to new ideas. By sleeping in front of the TV, we are giving the advertising world tremendous access to the deeper levels of our consciousness.

Other times when we are also very open are right before we go to sleep and in the morning, right before we wake up. These are very good times to program ourselves. They are times when we are in what is called the hypnogogic state. This is a state of consciousness when we are in a light trance.

As we are preparing for sleep, our minds are withdrawing from the external stimulation of the world. We are very open to internal stimulation. At that time, we can program ourselves by saying positive things.

Be very careful about what you say to yourself right before you go to sleep. It is very common for people, as they lie in bed at night, to think about all the unpleasant things that happened that day. They think about their problems or how bad they feel about themselves. If you do this, you are bringing up negative images that serve as suggestions and reminders to the subconscious mind. I guarantee that you will not be helping yourself to a comfortable sleep.

I believe that this explains one of the beneficial aspects of prayer. People who pray at night or before they go to bed thank God and forgive themselves and others. They typically ask for the best for themselves and for their loved ones. This is a powerful way of giving themselves very positive suggestions right before going to sleep.

I would suggest that, if you are religious, you continue that activity. If you are more secular, then make up your own "prayer." Make up a script that you can say to yourself at night before going to sleep. Think of it as a kind of prayer where you can thank the world, yourself, and those around you for a good life and for nurturing you.

It is also important to prepare yourself for the next day. Give yourself positive messages and images of what you will do and how you will feel the next morning. Visualize yourself getting up feeling refreshed, happy and energized. See yourself going through your morning routine such as showering and dressing. Then see yourself enthusiastically doing your creative work.

MORE ADVANCED PROGRAMMING

Hypnosis follows the laws of conditioning. It is like other learned behavior. You can condition yourself to deepen the level of hypnosis by following the rules of conditioning. One of these rules is that repetition strengthens the conditioned response. Repetition makes a learned response more difficult to extinguish (unlearn or remove). In addition, the more you practice relaxation, the more easily and deeply you will go into the relaxation state.

Writing programming scripts

With the deep relaxation script I have given you, you have now learned to access the deeper layers of your mind. It is now time to write a programming script. This second script will contain powerful messages for communicating with your deeper consciousness.

Write this script down on paper first. It should be about two or three handwritten pages (approximately a five- to ten-minute recording). After you compose it, you can record it on the opposite side of your relaxation tape and use this as a sequence. First, listen to the relaxation side of your tape and then listen to your programming script.

As you write your programming script, be specific. Take a small area in which you want to work. For example, do you need to overcome a specific fear? Do you have trouble handling a specific anxiety? Do you need to learn to say no when you are being disrespected? Do you need more energy and enthusiasm for your work? These are all potential areas for script writing and reprogramming. If you need more information about specific areas to work on, read over Chapters 4, 5 and 6.

Take one area of concern and write a full script for that area. Record that script and work with it for about one month. Then, take another area of concern and repeat the process. Now, you'll be working with two scripts. When you feel that you've mastered the method, move on to another area of concern. After a while, you will have four, five or more different scripts. Later on in this chapter I'll show you how all these scripts can be short-circuited through the use of anchoring and *symbolic words*. Use one or two scripts for two or three months before going on to another one or two scripts.

Creating powerful messages

To create powerful scripts, follow these rules:

1. Use vivid imagery. A picture is worth a thousand words, so paint as many pictures as possible. The more pictures, the better. Make these images as specific and detailed as possible. The more specific and detailed, the more powerful these images will be. Rather than saying "I get up in the

morning and start working," say "I see myself walking into my office. I sit at my oak desk, in my comfortable swivel chair. I use my favorite purple, ball point pen and begin writing on my blue letterhead."

2.   Use the present tense. Create the image of what you want to be but create it as if you are already there in the present time. Say "I am talking to Peter about . . ." not "I will talk to Peter about."

3.   Be as simple and direct as possible. Remember, we are tapping into the subconscious, childlike mind. Use simple and direct words, not fancy intellectual language or complicated concepts.

4.   Be emotional and dramatic in your script. Use words such as *exciting, great, amazing, fantastic,* and *wonderful.* The more the images are invested with emotional energy, the more impact they will have. Repeat the images and phrases in as many different ways as possible. Really see the images and feel the feelings.

5.   Be positive. For example, if you are working on procrastination, do not focus on a negative image of procrastination because that will only reinforce your procrastination by reminding you of it. When you use the word procrastination, it's hard not to form a picture of it in your mind. It's like saying, "Don't think of pink elephants." In order to avoid thinking about something, you have to think about it in order to avoid it. Instead, focus on the positive behavior you want to have. Regarding procrastination, concentrate on how energetic you are and how much you accomplish. Say "I take things as they come along and deal with them immediately. I am very productive."

Here are a few powerful and positive messages you could include in your scripts: "I am enjoying being creative. I am open and take risks. I see myself modifying and changing things. I love change." Repeat these images and phrases in as many different ways as possible. Really see the images and feel the feelings.

6. Reward yourself. In your script and in your imagination, see yourself doing the things you would like to do: being creative, writing a letter, writing a song, dancing for an audience, supervising a group of workers, selling a product. Then see yourself enjoying the accomplishment. Dramatize your enjoyment. See yourself laughing and feeling good, or being rewarded by others. Think big. See yourself getting a Grammy, or an Oscar or being applauded by an audience.

7. Symbolize the script. Give it a title, one word or short phrase that summarizes the whole script. Use a symbolic word or phrase so that it triggers the images in your mind. It could be a simple word such as sell or dance or a phrase such as great sale or fantastic dancer.

Short circuiting

Eventually, after many repetitions, you will be able to short-circuit your relaxation script. In other words, you will not need the whole script to get the same effect. Here's how short-circuiting works. You will learn certain key words that you associate with your script. This is called *anchoring* in Neuro Linguistic Programming. These key words will then begin to elicit the same responses that you are now getting with the full script. A few key words then will be enough to produce the effect of full programming. Finally, you will have a key word or phrase that *symbolizes* the whole experience and that will be enough to get you into that completely relaxed state. Eventually, you will learn not only to reduce these scripts by using the key word, but you can also link these different scripts together.

But for now, use this entire script and repeat it frequently, I would suggest that you repeat it at least once a day.

AFFIRMATIONS

Affirmations are short messages that we can create to empower ourselves. They are effective when said at anytime but most powerful when repeated over and over during a period of deep relaxation. Here are some positive affirmations you can start with.

Use your creativity to create affirmations to fit your specific needs.

1.   I am becoming more creative with each passing day.

2.   I feel part of a larger whole which creates through me.

3.   I believe that I am unique and original.

4.   I deserve to be happy.

5.   With each passing day, I get better at doing what I love best.

6.   My intuition is becoming stronger the more I trust it.

COULD THIS BE MAGIC?

Hypnosis, Neuro Linguistic Programming and visualization are powerful techniques when used properly and over a period of time. In some instances, they produce magical results.

Magic is a name we give to events that are mysterious and inexplicable by logic or science. Miracles occur against all known odds. We have already talked about miracle cures such as spontaneous healing. Patients sometimes regain the use of paralyzed limbs or have their eyesight restored with the use of hypnosis.

Depth psychologist Carl Jung coined the term *synchronicity* to describe "meaningful coincidences" that occur in life. For example, synchronicity occurred when, on the same day that my friend Gila decided she wanted to learn more about Australian aborigines, she received a flyer by mail announcing an Australian aborigine tribal music concert. Another example was when Frank, one of my students, had a dream about being on an alien ship and, the next day, received an invitation to join the Society for the Study of UFOs!

These examples suggest that there is a connection between seemingly unrelated events in the universe. Because of this connection, or as a reflection of the relationship, they occur simultaneously or in close proximity to each other. They are synchronized.

Pay attention to the meaningful coincidences in your life. I do. When I experience this phenomenon, it makes me realize how connected we are to each other and to the mysteries of the universe.

CONCLUSION

As you apply the methods outlined in this chapter, you too will discover the magic and power of autosuggestion and visualization. The more you believe in magic the more it is likely to occur. Just one caution: don't use "magical thinking" to avoid hard work. Don't wait for magic to happen. Make it happen with hard work.

In the following chapters we will explore additional methods to further enhance your creativity. You will also learn to use these procedures to tap into hidden resources in your subconscious mind. For example, you will learn to increase your "selling power" and to protect the Warrior from rejection and harsh criticism.

EXERCISES

★ 1. Examine your earliest beliefs. What is the very first memory you have? Relax and let yourself drift into the past until you find that time. Who is with you? What kind of a relationship do you have with them? What expectations do you have? What can you learn about your early beliefs at this stage?

★ 2. Have you ever had a magical experience? Recall an experience when something inexplicable occurred. Write or record a description of this experience in detail. Include all your sensory memories (sight, smell, touch, hear, taste) as well as your emotional reactions. Then write a script regarding your belief in magic.

★ 3. Pretend you are in a dangerous situation. You and your family are about to be destroyed. Your only chance for escape is to use your creativity. Find a way out before it's too late. When you do, write out the whole script, paying close attention to any feelings of triumph, power, relief, conquest, transformation and brilliance you feel.

★ 4. Write out a script that you can use at night just before going to sleep. Include thanks for your blessings and forgiveness for your limitations. Ask for things you want for yourself and those you love.

★ 5. Come up with three powerful affirmations that you can use to bolster your creativity.

★ 6. Examine what you say to yourself in your most relaxed states of mind. For example, what do you say to yourself right before falling asleep? Make sure you program yourself with positive thoughts. This is a state of consciousness in which suggestions from self talk can become deeply embedded.

★ 7. How often do you fall asleep in front of the TV set? Be aware that you are especially vulnerable during those times to accepting suggestions especially from advertisements.

★ 8. Become aware of your inner dialogue. Notice how often you program yourself with negative messages. How often do you program yourself with positive thoughts and words of encouragement?

CHAPTER 8

THE PLAYGROUND OF THE MIND

Visualization is not just an idea; it is one half of consciousness. It is one way we think, perhaps the more basic way.
Don Gerard, co-publisher of
Seeing with the Mind's Eye

IMAGERY AND VISUALIZATION

In the last chapter, we learned about deep relaxation and the creation of scripts for self-programming. We also explored the process by which pictures influence our subconscious mind. In this chapter, we will look further into the power of pictures and images for producing psychic change. We will examine the process called visualization. Visualization can be a passive process as in meditation, or an active process, as in guided imagery.

Using visualization is just like using electricity: you don't have to know exactly how it works to use it effectively.
Valerie Wells,
The Joy of Visualization

In meditation, images are allowed to emerge spontaneously from deep within our subconscious mind. For example, during meditation we are in a relaxed and receptive state of mind. Spontaneously, images come up that can then be examined or interpreted. Using this passive approach, we learn a great deal about our unconscious thoughts and desires.

An active approach to visualization is to direct our consciousness to specified images. We have already done this in our programming scripts. As you recall from chapter 7, Rule #2 encouraged you to use vivid imagery. The more detailed and specific the pictures, the more powerful the images and the more you are using your active imagination.

One technique that uses active imagination for growth and self-understanding is *guided imagery*. In guided imagery you use your "mind's eye" to explore various situations in an imaginary world. For example, imagine yourself on a vacation in the Bahamas. Now, imagine yourself doing something you've always fantasized about such as scuba diving or parasailing. Can you clearly visualize yourself? If so, you have just used your active imagination and I have just guided you to use images in your mind's eye.

The more vivid the images, the more powerful your visualizations will be. And the more you can involve your five senses in your visualizations, the better your images will be. So, let's begin with the following sensory exercises to help you use each sense for visualization.

1.   Use your memory to visualize an apple. Think about the last time you actually saw an apple. See the colors and textures. Get as clear an image as you can. Really examine the apple in detail and from every angle.

2.   Use your memory again to remember a sound, such as a train passing by, thunder, or rain. Recall as much detail of that sound as possible. How distant or close was it? How loud? How sweet or piercing? Use as many words as you can to describe the sound.

3.   Recall a particularly strong smell. It could be a flower, food or perfume. It could also be a foul odor. Remember your reaction and how you felt physically when you smelled it.

4. Next, chose something you have tasted and recall that experience. Pay close attention to the physical memory. How did it taste on your tongue?

5. Finally, recall a tactile sensation. This would be something you touched or that touched you in a significant and compelling manner. Recall how it felt on your skin. What part of your body was involved? What was the sensation like?

Now that you have done these sensory exercises, you will have enhanced your ability to create vivid images by engaging your five senses. This skill will be a great asset to you in the more advanced visualizations that follow.

You have been using your memory to recall actual events. Now, let's practice visualization using your active imagination. Do this by creating images that you may have not previously experienced. For example, use your active imagination to visualize:

1. Two lovers sitting on a park bench.

2. Yourself sketching a human face.

3. A piano in your living room.

We can also visualize images that don't exist in the external world (as far as we know). It will take a little more imagination to conjure up these images. Visualize:

1. A purple people-eater.

2. An animal that's half horse, half rabbit.

3. A house made out of chocolate or cotton candy.

4. A machine that can predict the future.

Wasn't that fun? Create more images on your own. Free up your imagination. Give it free reign to fantasize and create whatever you please.

IMAGINATION: OUR MOST UNLIMITED RESOURCE

Children are very good at using their imaginations. They do it naturally. So what is imagination? I like the definition of Gestalt psychologist Edward Tolman, who called imagination *vicarious trial and error learning*. In the "real" world, we deal with objects that we can manipulate and interact with directly. Vicarious, on the other hand, means that we are not dealing with objects directly, but with images or representations of those objects. So, vicarious trial and error learning means that we are not manipulating the world directly. Rather, we are using images and representations to interact with the world. In fact, most of our learning occurs vicariously. That's what allows us, as humans, to develop so much more rapidly and extensively than "lower" animals. Apparently, lower animals have little or no imagination; therefore, what they learn about the world is done mainly through direct interaction with it.

Children also learn through direct interaction with the world. But most of our learning after childhood occurs vicariously. As we learn to have symbols (images and representations) of the world, we are no longer limited to learning by direct interaction with the world. We can now grow by manipulating symbols. Our learning, therefore, accelerates at a tremendous rate. It is this imagination, this ability to manipulate symbols, consciously and unconsciously, that gives us our tremendous ability to be highly creative.

Unfortunately, most of us learn to devalue the imagination and, through disuse, we lose it. We become reality oriented, logical and rational, thus depriving ourselves of a fantastic resource for creativity.

That's the bad news. The good news is that we can recover this great resource. By allowing ourselves to roam around in our imaginations, we can make new connections and new associations. We must give ourselves permission to fantasize and have fun with our imaginations in order to tap into this fountain of images and ideas.

Many of us were ridiculed at an early age for using too much fantasy or for not being able to tell the difference between fantasy and reality. In fact, part of our early socialization was learning to distinguish between imagination and reality.

My client Albert is an excellent example of childhood creativity lost and found. At age nine, Albert loved to play with toy spacemen for hours on end. He imagined himself and his crew going on missions to Mars. When his crew encountered a survival problem, they solved it using an imaginary computer. Albert's older brother, Paul, however, constantly reminded him that he was too old to play with toy space soldiers. He ridiculed him regularly. Under pressure, Albert finally gave up playing with space toys and learned to devalue his childhood imagination in the process. Many years later he reported that he was bored in his job and that his life was dull. Not until he rediscovered the child within was he able to recover the joy of playing in an imaginary world.

It is common to see children play by themselves. They are comfortable in their imaginary worlds and can entertain themselves for hours and hours without losing interest. Only when the child has learned to devalue the imagination does he becomes easily bored. And when too much emphasis is placed on being realistic or logical, imagination is stifled.

In the world of imagination there is no need to be logical. The unconscious mind makes free associations and combines things in a very illogical way. For people who have a strong need to be logical, this is a problem. They are uncomfortable using too much imagination and fantasy. So, again, the function and the process of imagination are depreciated. Being imaginative has less value than being realistic.

SEEING WITH THE MIND'S EYE

The ability to visualize is central to the creative process. The painter visualizes her model when she's not directly in front of her. The writer must be able to vividly visualize his characters in order to get into the story and move it along.

Visualization can also be useful when we are writing a letter to a friend or a prospective client. By visualizing that person reading our letter, as we write down the words we interject an intimacy and directness that would otherwise be missing. By visualizing their reactions and modifying our letter accordingly, we increase the effectiveness of our communication.

It is a well-established fact that visualization prior to a performance improves one's actual performance. Baseball great, Kirk Gibson, is only one of the multitude of athletes that uses visualization. He is quoted in the May 27, 1995 sports section of the *Los Angeles Times* as saying, "That's what the battle's all about, hanging in until I can find something to hit. When I go up, I *visualize* {emphasis mine} coming through. I think about the last time I had success."

A classic research study on mental practice done by psychologist Alan Richardson further demonstrates the value of visualization. A group of boys who imagined sinking basketballs into the basket improved their performance almost as much as a control group of boys who physically practiced making free throws every day for twenty days!

Now let's further explore guided imagery and use our powers of visualization to uncover our hidden resources.

GUIDED VISUALIZATIONS

The following exercises use visualization to stimulate your imagination and reunite you with valuable parts of your psyche. To get the most out of these exercises, do them when you are relaxed. Find a place where you have some privacy and will not be interrupted. Create a space where you can let your imagination run wild.

The Goal

This visualization will help you clarify your goals and become more focused. While in a deeply relaxed state, imagine that you have just received a phone call about making a trip. Who is calling you? Visualize this person clearly. Where do they want you to go? Ask them why they want you to make this journey, then ask for more details. How long will the journey take? Who would go with you? What do you need to bring along? Visualize the journey. Is it going to be on water, on air or on land? During what season will it take place? In what country?

At the end of your visualization, let your caller know whether you are willing to take on this venture. If you are not ready, express what else you will need to make your decision. If you are ready, tell your caller what you need and want in the way of support, supplies and incentives.

The Creative Journey

Visualize yourself taking a creativity journey. First say to yourself, "I want to experience my deepest thoughts and feelings about developing my creativity."

See yourself start off on your journey. Where are you going? What are you taking on your trip? What form of transportation are you using? Use your senses to experience these aspects of the journey. As you take off, ask yourself, "What am I feeling? Do I have any misgivings? Do I have fears? What am I most optimistic about?"

Take the journey. As you continue on your journey, you meet up with some people with whom you talk. They advise you about what's ahead. Note their advice. Find some allies that will go with you at least part of the way.

The Key

Visualize a key that will be your secret tool for opening up creativity doors. It is a key that will change its size and shape to fit whatever problem needs a solution. Hold the key in your hand. Feel it, see it and talk to it. Now ask it to help you with a particular problem so you may test its power. Go ahead and unlock the secret to solving a dilemma. Or use it to unlock the treasures hidden in your subconscious mind.

The Block

Something is keeping you from fulfilling your dreams. Visualize this obstacle. What are its dimensions? What is it made of? Smell it, touch it, feel it, hear it. Talk to it. Ask it to reveal its reasons for blocking you. Is it to punish you? To pay you back for something you feel guilty about? What will make it go away?

Be creative and find different ways of removing the block. Perhaps you could reframe your conception of this block. For example, if it is a wall, remember that not all walls are negative. The walls in a house are very useful for keeping out the rain, the wind and unwanted pollution. Some walls are painted with murals and are quite beautiful.

If all else fails, summon your allies to help you. Ask them to help you remove this block. Have strategy meetings with them. Muster all your skills and forces. Make the block transparent. Ask yourself, "Do I need to go around it, over it or destroy it?" or "What's on the other side?"

After the block is removed or transcended, celebrate your accomplishment. Feel the freedom. Enjoy the newfound energy. Thank your helpers and revel in your creativity.

MOVIES IN YOUR HEAD

As you become more familiar with the technique of visualization, you will realize the power of this vicarious trial and error tool. Use it to create movies in your head. Write your own scripts and scenarios and solve problems by visualizing. Here are a few more examples of how visualizations can expand your imagination.

A Visualization for Managers

You are having a problem with one of your workers. How can you get this worker to stop coming in late, taking too many breaks or harassing a coworker? First visualize a solution to this problem. Look deep within yourself to find an answer that both solves the problem and elicits the worker's cooperation in implementing the solution.

Now visualize yourself talking to that worker. Don't embarrass or humiliate him. To help him save face, don't talk to him in front of his coworkers. Communicate your concerns and present him with the problem and any possible solutions. Have him participate in finding the solution. See yourself having a meeting in which genuine communication is taking place.

Where is this meeting taking place? How are you dressed? What is your body language? Does your tone of voice invite communication? Is the worker becoming defensive? If so, set him at ease. See yourself relaxed and in control. You are confident that you will get the job done effectively and completely. Feel the positive atmosphere in your meeting. You have rapport with your worker. He is listening to you because he understands your desire to solve the problem rather than punish him. Thank him for his cooperation. Now prepare all the details of your communication with him. Decide on the exact time this meeting will take place.

When you meet with the employee imagine that you have already communicated with him. Expect that he will be cooperative and that you will reach a satisfactory resolution to the problem.

The Traveling Laboratory

In Chapter 6, you established a physical place where you do most of your creating. We called that your Creativity Center. Now we will create a similar space in your imagination where you can go any time you feel like creating. I call this my Traveling Laboratory, but feel free to call it anything you like. Some alternatives are:

- The Imagineering Center

- The Mental Workshop

- Free Space

- Creative Space

The Traveling Laboratory (TL) is a place where you can experiment with ideas and concepts. You can create in this workplace while sitting in the doctor's office, waiting in line, or doing a task that does not require your full attention. In this way you can devote many additional hours to your creativity.

Begin creating your TL by imagining a space in your head. Look inside and explore this space. Is it dark or light? Make it as big as you like. You can increase or decrease its size at will depending on your needs. For example, if you are involved in some other task while you are in your TL, decrease its size to allow you to devote mental energies to your other task. The more complex your other task, the more you need to decrease the space in your laboratory.

Likewise, if you are not involved in any other task and need more resources for your laboratory, increase its size to infinity! Your imagination has no limit. What do you see now? Play with this for a while, increasing and decreasing your laboratory's size.

Now look at the contents of your TL. What do you see? Give yourself permission to bring in any tool you need whenever you need it. Next time you are working on a problem or reviewing material for your creative projects, go into the laboratory and work for as long as you want with whatever tool you want. When done, you may want to put out the light in your laboratory until you need it again. Alternately, you may leave the light on and just diminish its size to allow you to work on other projects. Encourage your unconscious to keep working in your laboratory until you return.

Capturing Lightning in a Bottle

Imagine that you are holding a bottle in your hand, a bottle you will use to capture some creative lightning. The night is filled with thunder and lightning. The lightning illuminates the night sky in a magnificent display of energy and light. See the cracks in the sky and the spectacular fireworks produced by the lightning. You are filled with inspiration and ideas that rumble about in your superconscious mind. Now hold out the bottle to capture the lightning. Or perhaps, as Benjamin Franklin did with his key, you want to place your bottle on the tail of a kite to send up to the lightning-filled sky.

See the lightning as you hold out your bottle and fill it up. It shines brightly and illuminates everything. You bring it closer to you and you pour it into yourself. As it enters your body, you feel electrified. Your head is filled with blinding white light. It's so intense you can't even look at it. Thoughts and images are rushing through your mind. New ideas and insights are pouring out of you. You don't know the meaning of every one of these images and insights at this time, but eventually you will.

The Anxiety Bag

Relaxation is important in managing moment-to-moment anxiety during creative work. When you find yourself becoming tense or confused, simply take a few deep breaths and clear your head. Think and say the word "clear."

Once you have become proficient with the relaxation process described in Chapter 7, you can use it anytime, anyplace. You can choose the level of relaxation you wish to achieve and can attain that level instantly.

Another excellent way to manage anxiety is with the anxiety bag. Here's how it works. Visualize blowing into a brown paper bag. (No, it doesn't have to be brown. Chose any color your wish. Perhaps a relaxing color, like pink, would be better for you.) As you blow into the bag, see all your unproductive worries and anxieties going into it. Feel how this relieves you physically. Feel how you can breathe more easily and have more pleasure in your body.

Now take the bag and tie it up securely. Don't worry, your anxieties will not go away (unless you want them to). You are merely storing them temporarily. When you are ready to take them back in, simply open up the bag and breathe them in!

The anxiety bag is an especially useful technique for handling annoying worries that keep us from our work and for dealing with procrastination in general. It's also a great way to get a good night's sleep. Do it right before you want to start working or right before going to bed.

The Affect Bridge

The affect bridge is a technique used to bring a feeling from the past back into the present. You can also use the bridge to take that feeling into the future. I learned the basics of this technique from Dr. Eleanor Field, a clinical psychologist and director of Professional Associates in Clinical Hypnotherapy in Tarzana, California. Here's how it works:

Get into a deep state of relaxation. Then get in touch with a feeling of creativity in your present life. Now take that feeling back to an earlier time in your life when you were also creative. Do this by visualizing yourself taking a trip. Choose whatever mode of transportation you like. It could be a train, a time machine, or a magic carpet. Here are some images that will make it easier for you to travel to your past:

1. Go upstairs to the attic of your past.

2. See the pages of a calendar come back onto the calendar one by one as you go back in time.

3. Visualize a clock with the hands of time going backwards.

Now you are going back to a time and place when you were very creative. Perhaps you were a child and playing with toys. Maybe you were doodling or doing finger painting. In this place you felt free and uninhibited. Your imagination was rich and vivid. You felt totally secure and absorbed in your play.

As you return to this place and time, let yourself experience all the associated sensations and emotions. Relive the feelings. Experience the fun and the pleasure. Take a few minutes to do this.

As you relive this experience, look around. Take note of your surroundings. Then look inside. Take note of your physical sensations as well as your thoughts and feelings. Who is with you? What are you playing with? What is your energy level? What are the essential ingredients that make up this experience?

When you get ready to leave this place, you will enjoy it one more time before parting with your toys. If there is a playmate (or playmates) with you, tell them you will be back. Where in your body do you feel this experience the strongest? Touch yourself there. Next time you want to reexperience this feeling, touch yourself in the same place. Give yourself permission to come back whenever you want to.

Now come back to the present using the same mode of transportation you used in your journey back in time. Remember what you have just experienced. Remember the feelings, sensations and emotions associated with the experience of freedom and spontaneity, the experience of heightened creativity. Let these sensations, feelings and emotions become totally absorbed by your mind and body. Remember the essential ingredients of the experience. Make this creativity experience part of your present self. Be confident that you have regained your creative energies. From this day forward, you will feel this confidence in your everyday creativity.

When you feel ready, project yourself into the future. Go to any place you would like to be or any stage you would like to be at in one of your creative projects. You can use any mode of transportation you wish at this point. Be sure to bring the essential ingredients you have just experienced from the past with you. Now see yourself using what you have brought along in working on your project. Note the date in the future when you are doing this.

FINAL NOTE

Creative visualizations will have powerful effects on you if you let them. Properly done, they will transform your life. Your new perceptions, images and feelings will become part of your nervous system and affect your muscle tension, heart rate, body chemistry and even your hormonal levels. Scientific studies have shown that images can control blood pressure, respiratory rate and metabolism.

Slowly over a period of time, you will open new doors to your imagination. You will discover long-buried treasures and unused resources.

Allow yourself to be dramatic in your images. Let your imagination conjure up bizarre and fantastic images that can release the primordial energies of your unconscious. Talk to Mozart or Ben Franklin about their creative process. Ask Bill Gates about the secrets of his success or spend time with Mother Theresa learning about the source of her compassion and love.

By practicing visualization, you will learn that our only true limitations reside in our imaginations.

PRACTICE

1. Visualize your inner voice. What does it sound like? Tell it how important it is for you to hear it and why. Ask it to help you.

2. Imagine dropping a tape in a mailbox and asking your subconscious to deliver it to you tomorrow with answers to your dilemmas.

3. Use the affect bridge to reconnect present feelings and emotions with similar feeling and emotions in your past.

Remember to reconnect feelings and emotions and not just ideas and thoughts. Reconnect with:

a. Your most creative moment.
b. A moment when you received lavish praise for being creative.
c. A moment you achieved great personal satisfaction from your creativity.

4. Your mind is like a rain cloud or a fertile garden. Visualize each of these images. How are they like your creative imagination? For example, the rain cloud is about to burst and each raindrop is an idea that you can capture for your creative project. Or the garden must be fertilized and seeds planted before flowers can grow. Visualize these two images in detail. Watch the rain come down or the seeds sprout. Imagine that the raindrops or the flowers are your new ideas. Talk to these images and tell them what you need or intend to do to be creative.

5. Rate your images according to how vivid they are. Do this for different modalities. For example, how vivid are your auditory images? Your olfactory (smell) images? Your tactile (touch) images? Make it a point to practice in order to improve the vividness of each modality.

CHAPTER 9

PUMPING UP YOUR CREATIVE MUSCLES

We cannot will to have insights. We cannot will to have creativity. But we can will to give ourselves to the creative experience with intensity of dedication and commitment.

Rollo May,
The Courage to Create

In this and the next two chapters I will provide you with a variety of strategies, tactics and devices to stimulate your creativity. You might also think of them as maneuvers, schemes, procedures, techniques, games, exercises or tools that you can put in your creativity tool box.

The creativity strategies in these three chapters are divided into three categories. This chapter describes the tools that are used primarily in the analysis part of the creative process. In Chapter 10 are those tools that are more commonly used in the *synthesis* or putting together part of creativity. Keep in mind that this division is somewhat arbitrary. For instance, a solution can be discovered while using an analysis tool.

Also keep in mind that a particular tool can be used in several stages of a creative project. It is not always possible to know at what stage a particular tool will be used. The best approach is to understand these strategies and then experiment with them. Use them anywhere and everywhere. Use them for analysis and/or synthesis. Try them at any time during your creative process. Be sensitive to the demands of the problem. Let the problem lead you to the right tools. Over time you will make these tools your own and incorporate them into your handy and immediately accessible tool kit.

Finally, in Chapter 11, I describe methods that involve a change in language. Thus we can get a fresh perspective on our work by learning to express and describe our situations in an unfamiliar language system. We will look at the language of dance, of drawing and of music as three separate modes of knowing.

GETTING STARTED

It has been said that creativity involves *finding* problems as much as solving them. Test this out. Look around your workplace for problems. A good rule of thumb is to look in areas that pique your curiosity. If something fascinates you, chances are there is some interesting tension there that is worth investigating for creativity projects.

Defining a problem is 50 percent of the solution. Take time to think about your project and how best to define its problems. The definition of the problem becomes the center around which everything else revolves. For example, songwriters often start with the title of a song. A title defines the issues in a song and gives a central focus. The title is something that "hooks" the audience and is the highlight of the song. It also suggests the conflict of the story and its resolution. It is the acorn from which the tree will grow. Think of songs like "Just the Two of Us," "The Wind Beneath My Wings" and "Girls Just Want to Have Fun." These songs "write themselves" because the titles hold a wealth of information and summarize the messages of the songs.

A mission statement for an organization serves a similar role. It focuses the group's activities and goals around a central theme. As problems arise in the organization, members can use the statements of purpose as a focal point for defining strategies and creating solutions.

In creativity, we often change our definition of a problem as we proceed in a project. This flexibility is good. However, it is also worthwhile to take some extra time at the beginning of our project to choose the right problem to solve *before* proceeding. For example, if you're stressed out, you may think that going on a vacation in the Bahamas is the answer. Upon closer examination, however, you could discover that you just want to lie on the beach and not have to worry about cooking, cleaning or work. The problem to be solved is a need for worry-free relaxation. By redefining the problem, you may decide that going down to a nice motel at the local beach can satisfy your need as fully as going all the way to the Bahamas. You'll have the added bonus of saving money and time for some other project.

RESEARCH

One of the main purposes of research is to find out what has been done before. Researching will lead you to new ideas and ways of modifying old methods. Collect newspaper articles. Browse bookstores or the library. Interview people, go online, hold focus groups, read, watch TV. Travel. Go to your idea book. You have one by now, don't you?

Gather your information and organize it. Use your computer to create files or make folders and file them in your filing cabinet. Research and organization are crucial at all levels of the creative process, not only in the beginning stages. As the project develops, additional research will need to be done. Having your prior research catalogued and labeled will allow you to easily find the information you need when you need it.

The artist is a receptacle for emotions that come from all over the place; from the sky, from the earth, from a scrap of paper, from a passing shape, from a spider's web.
Picasso

LISTS AND SKETCHES

Keep paper handy for jotting down thoughts and ideas throughout the day. Lists are good time management tools. "To do" lists are essential to keeping ourselves organized and focused. They help move us from "planning" to "doing." Prioritize your things to do and check them off after you do them. When you come up with a new thing to do or finish something and don't have your list handy, jot it down on any piece of paper and add or delete it from your list later on.

I learned the importance of lists a few years ago when I was producing the Latin Music Expo in Los Angeles. Each evening I made a list of things to do and people to call the following day. Every morning I went through my list and checked items off as they were done. The list was essential to the success of the event in several ways. For one, the list helped to manage my anxiety. Because I didn't have to keep everything in memory, I didn't worry about forgetting to do something. Secondly, it was a basic organizational and communications tool. Once I had put things down on the list, I could think about what wasn't yet on it. Then I could prioritize my activities. It also served as an outline for comparing notes with other organizers and seeing what was being left out. Thirdly, it concretized my accomplishments. Tangibly seeing what I had completed provided me with a reward for the time and energy I had spent that day. Last, but not least, the list helped me organize the following day's work and make an accurate assessment of the overall progress I was making on the event.

Sketches are an excellent way of organizing your work and thinking on paper. Taking measurements, creating designs, sketching outlines or drawing pictures are ways of envisioning what your final product will be. These can be actual blueprints or dreams and fantasies. The creative uses of drawing will be discussed in detail in Chapter 10.

OUTLINING AND CLUSTERING

Remember outlining in school? Roman numerals, followed by subheadings in capital letters, followed by sub-subheadings in

Arabic numerals? As in many cases, your teacher may have taught this technique in a very rigid, authoritarian manner and turned you off to its practical usefulness. Turn yourself back on to this valuable tool. Outlining is an excellent way of organizing your work. It breaks down tasks into components and organizes the work into a logical sequence. An outline also subdivides a problem by putting items into levels of importance or specificity.

Recently, *radial outlining and clustering* have become popular ways of organizing material in a less linear fashion. Another name for this process of making nonlinear outlines is *idea mapping*. Using these methods, you spin out a web of ideas tied together by interconnecting lines. The web is circular or radial and the ideas are grouped in clusters.

The following example is a description of idea mapping in a business setting. The problem is how to improve office productivity.

1. In the center of a page, put down a word or phrase that best describes the problem you are working on. In this case, it's "Office Productivity."

2. Next, use fast, free association to come up with related words. Do not censor or judge prematurely. Write associated words down anywhere around the main word. (Refer to Figure 2.)

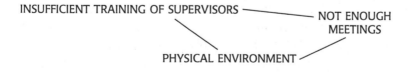

Figure 2. Office Productivity: Free Association

3. Draw lines to connect any of the words or phrases that appear to be related. Figure 2 shows lines connecting words that involve employees relating to each other such as "power struggles" and "jealousy." These connected, related words are called clusters. Figure 2 shows two clusters of interconnected words.

4. Think of a word that best describes and conceptualizes each cluster. These concepts may already be written down in your web of words. If not, write them down. Put a geometrical figure such as a star, square or circle around these concepts. These concepts are like your different levels in a conventional, linear outline. Each geometric shape corresponds to a level such as the Roman numeral level, the capital letter level, the Arabic number level, etc.

Here's where your outline will help you think through your creation. In this case, I had connected "jealousies," "drugs," and "power struggles." I could see that the words in this cluster all referred to employee relationship problems, so I created my first concept, "employee behavior problems." I put a star around this concept. I could also see that my other cluster of interconnected words dealt with "management/organizational problems." I created that as my second concept and put a star around it also. See Figure 3.

As I did this, I realized that I had many problems but no solutions. This led me to create and write down a concept called "solutions" to contrast with the two problem concepts. See figure 4. I then saw that "problems" and "solutions" were my main concepts and that the other two concepts would be subsumed under them. I put a square around "problems" and a square around "solutions." My outline was now getting too cluttered. I took a new sheet of paper and reorganized the outline.

I could now put down some words under "solutions." Since the solutions were directly related to the problems I had analyzed, I used the same words under "solutions" that I had used under "problems." Thus, as shown in Figure 4, the concept "solutions" could include "employee solutions" and "management/organiza-

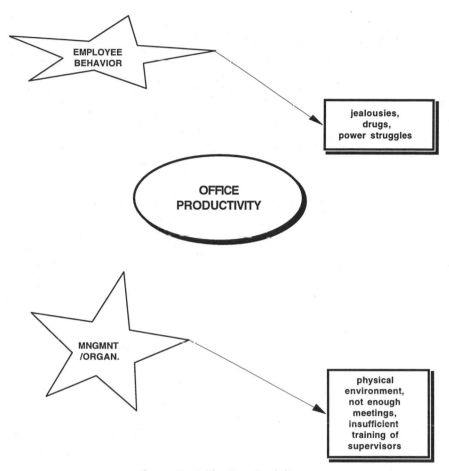

Figure 3. Office Productivity

tional solutions." Notice that these two concepts under "solutions" are enclosed in a star since they are on the same level as the same concepts under "problems."

5. Take the remaining ideas (the ones with no geometric shapes around them) and see if they'll fit into the existing categories. If not, do they form a new category? If they do, make a new category and a new geometric shape for it. Continue expanding your outline, if necessary, following the process described in #4 above.

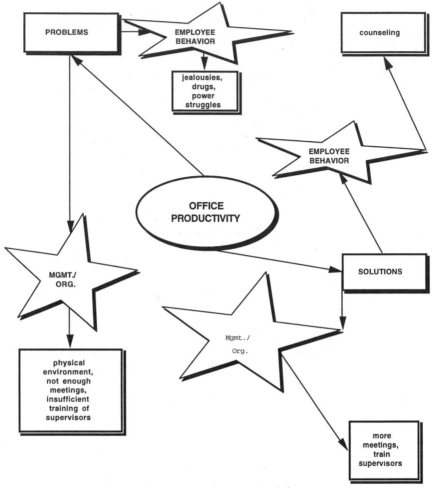

Figure 4. Office Productivity

When doing your maps and clusters, remember these basic rules:

1. Use a pencil rather than a pen. You'll probably do plenty of erasing.

2. Redo your diagram often. When it gets too cluttered, start on a new sheet of paper and reorganize your clusters.

3. Put new ideas near similar ideas.

4. Add a new concept whenever you recognize one.

5. Periodically, look at the broad groupings (categories) and try to identify a completely different grouping. Then, think of specific ideas that fit within that new grouping.

Many people prefer the radial method of outlining to the traditional linear approach because radial outlining is more fluid and flexible. It allows for brainstorming and free association. You can write words anywhere on the page as you start out and then organize as you go along.

After making this kind of outline, you can very easily create a more linear outline. To do this, arrange your clusters according to order of importance. Then label them using the traditional system described earlier of Roman numerals, capital letters, Arabic numerals, and lowercase letters. Figure 5 shows our example, "Office Productivity," in a linear outline.

Outlines may seem like a lot of work now, but be aware that after doing a few outlines on paper, you will be able to do them in your head!

OFFICE PRODUCTIVITY

I. Problems

    A. Mgmt./org.

        1. Physical environment

        2. Not enough meetings

        3. Insufficient training of supervisors

    B. Employee behavior

        1. Jealousies

        2. Drugs

        3. Power struggles

II. Solutions

    A. Mgmt./org.

        1. More meetings

        2. Train supervisors

    B. Employee behavior

        1. Counseling

Figure 5.

Radial outlines or idea maps can be expanded and used in a variety of ways. For more information on this creativity tool see Richard Fobe's *The Creative Problem Solver's Toolbox* and Charles "Chic" Thompson's *What a Great Idea!*

By the way, excellent computer software is available to help you in outlining. The program is called Inspiration and is put out by Inspiration Software, Inc. in Portland, Oregon (telephone: 503-207-3004). This software is helpful in making flow charts and presentation diagrams as well. The program allows you to create a variety of shapes, such as ovals, clouds and stars. It generates arrows to connect your shapes. Among other things, it will generate a linear outline from your idea map. Figures 2, 3, 4 and 5 were created using Inspiration software.

PERSPECTIVE: LEVELS, VIEWPOINTS AND ANGLES

It's entirely too easy to get into a fixed way of looking at a situation. To get a fresh look, we have to change our perspective.

The Buddhists teach us that we must use "beginner's mind" in order to see things as they really are. We must empty our minds to get beyond the illusions that block our vision. The beginner's mind lives in the "now." It is open and innocent. It is not filled with the preconceptions and prejudices of its opposite, the "expert mind."

Western philosophers called phenomenologists have similarly stated that, in order to see into the essence of reality, we must *adopt a naive consciousness.* Existentialists, such as Jean Paul Sartre, use the phenomcnologist's approach to try to understand Being (anything that is). Their approach is to "bracket" the world and try to see Being as it is, without labels and predetermined notions.

The hero in Robert Heinlein's novel *Stranger in a Strange Land* had a similar method of understanding. He tried to understand the true and deeper nature of things by "groking" them. His method involved becoming one with the object. He "groked" by suspending judgments and labels. In order to do this, he would focus, concentrate and become totally absorbed in the object.

Try "groking" your problem next time you get stuck and need a new perspective. Concentrate and become one with the problem, whether it is a painting, a story or a song you are working on. Take on a beginner's mind. Using the naive point of view, imagine that you are seeing this for the first time. Empty your mind and see the "thing-in-itself" without preconceived notions.

> *The most beautiful experience we can have is the myste-*
> *rious . . . He to whom the emotion is a stranger, who can*
> *no longer pause and stand wrapped in awe, is as good as*
> *dead; his eyes are closed.*
> **Albert Einstein**

Another way of getting a new perspective is to *imagine how another person might experience your situation* or problem. Make this other person someone you admire or someone who is the opposite of you. Or try someone who is much older or younger. I experienced a new perspective recently when I took my seven-year-old niece to Disneyland. I had been there many times before. The thrill was gone. It was becoming a drudgery to entertain out-of-town guests by taking them to the park. What a treat to see it through the eyes of a seven-year-old! Goofy, Mickey Mouse and all the Disney characters seemed so real and the night parade was magical.

Seeing the situation from the point of view of the object itself is very similar to "groking." If you are a salesperson, ask yourself: "How does the VCR feel when I am demonstrating it?" If you are packing a set of fragile china for shipping, ask yourself: "How do the dishes feel inside the crate and being moved about?"

John Lasseter, toy maker for the movie *Toys,* really studies his toys' lives before trying to create their personalities. He tries to understand how these toys will be treated by children and how the toy will feel, especially if the child no longer wants to play with it. In a *Los Angeles Times* article of November 19, 1995, David Kronke quotes him as saying, "So when you think of things that would cause anxiety in a toy's life, it would be the things that would prevent him from being played with by a child—he could be broken, stolen, lost, or he could be outgrown." Lassiter, therefore, creates his toys to minimize the chances of one of these things occurring.

Changing levels of abstraction can also give you a new perspective. Look at your object from a concrete level, then change to an abstract position. A particular apple is very different from an apple that is part of a group called fruit. When looking at a particular apple, we would notice its specific color, shading and size. As a member of a group called fruit, however, we might pay more attention to the fact that it grows on trees or plants or that it contains seeds or a pit.

Changing geographical levels is another way of getting a fresh look. There's nothing like taking a long trip away from your problems to put them in proper perspective. If you can't physically take a trip, use your imagination to do so. Visualize your problem as seen from another location. Perhaps you can look at it from the moon or from a beach in Bermuda.

The different ways in which we can change perspective are unending. In a classroom or meeting situation, change perspective by *changing the sitting arrangement.* See the world differently by wearing a hat, walking barefooted or taking the bus. See it from a different racial or cultural perspective. Turn the problem upside down, inside out or paint it a different color. Change its size, dimensions, texture, intensity. Neuro Linguistic Programming uses perspective to get rid of phobias and create personality change. A fear will look less threatening if we visualize it and then make it appear smaller, more distant or dimmer.

A real estate manager friend of mine solved his apartment rental problems by looking at the situation from a tenant's point of view. Earl was having a hard time renting his apartment units until he got into the prospective tenant's shoes. He then realized that many potential renters were being eliminated because so many apartments did not allow pets. Earl decided to allow pets and his vacancy rate dropped. But he went even further. He decided to put a kennel on the premises too. Tenants were delighted to have a place to leave their pets when they went out of town. Earl's apartments were in such demand, he was able to raise his rents and still have a full house! This particular example also illustrates the technique of combining unrelated items, to be discussed later.

DIVIDE AND SUBDIVIDE

Simplify a large problem by breaking it up into smaller components. An old adage says, "Every long journey begins with a single step." For example, if you are writing a book, break it up into chapters. Make a folder for each chapter and then collect all the information you need for each chapter in the respective folders. If you write one page a day, in one year, you'll have a 350-page book.

Similarly, a house is basically a set of rooms put together. Work on your plan for each room separately. Whether you're building a new house, remodeling or redecorating, simplify your task by breaking it into modules. Then put the modules together to get an overall view of your project.

ATTRIBUTE LISTING

Attribute listing is an excellent example of subdividing a problem into components. This technique involves two phases. The first phase is simply to list the attributes of an object or problem. For example, a bicycle can be broken down and analyzed into the following attributes:

1. Seat

2. Wheels

3. Handlebars

4. Frame

5. Is used for transportation

6. Can be romantic

7. Is popular on college campuses

8. Can be dangerous to ride, especially at night

In the second phase of the process, you change one or more of the attributes to create a new product or develop a new perspective on a problem. In our bicycle example, we could create a new product by making variations on some or all of the attributes. Each attribute could be assigned to a person or committee to see how it could be improved. They would also study the feasibility of making it more durable, less expensive or more aesthetic. Perhaps they could focus on the romantic attribute and make it more appealing to couples in love. This would be particularly useful in advertising the new product. The possibilities are enormous.

In general, here are some of the attributes that can be listed:

1. Physical. List the different parts and their qualities. Physical attributes include width, depth, length, weight, thickness, etc. They can also include distance, color, shade, texture and speed. Try changing intensity, temperature, location, smell or texture.

2. Manufacturing. Is it made by hand or on an assembly line? List the materials used and the process of putting the product together.

3. Marketing. How is the product sold? In stores, through mail order or at seminars and conferences? Can the packaging be changed? Can it be advertised and promoted in a new medium? Can the product be distributed through new channels? How about mail order or Internet marketing?

4. Uses. Can new uses for the product be found? Can it be used indoors, outdoors, by men or women, children or adults? Can a new group of people find a use for the product or service? Are there any unusual uses it can have?

Many creative products come about as a result of imitation and copying. Some musicians admit that their compositions came about by trying to copy a recording they greatly admired. They copied it badly in the sense that it wasn't exactly like the original. Unintentionally, they changed one or more attributes of what they copied and in doing so, created something new.

With attribute listing you can copy or modify more deliberately and intentionally. This technique has been successfully used by all the fast food restaurants that have copied McDonald's and photocopy stores capitalizing on the idea of PIP or KINKO'S.

MENTAL AEROBICS

Any verb in the dictionary can be used as a tool to stretch your conceptions and perspectives. Try these verbs on for size to see if they can give you a fresh angle on your creation: reverse, rearrange, combine, modify, substitute, experiment, twist, turn, flip, somersault, jump, pole vault, hurdle, stretch, bend, flex, scale, leap, display, question, reverse, compare, expand, freeze, eliminate, itemize, clarify.

It's probably easy to see what would happen if you "eliminated" or "rearranged" certain aspects of your solutions or if you "combined" it with something else. But what would it mean to "jump" or "explode" it?

OPPOSITES

Another mind-stretching game involves imagining opposites. Think about the opposite of what you are trying to accomplish. Identifying what you don't want may shed some light on what you do want. This technique often leads to humorous results that free us from rigid ways of thinking. For example, instead of trying to figure out how to make yourself happy, write an essay entitled "1001 Ways to Make Ourselves Miserable!"

A related technique is to first think of what is holding you back from reaching a solution and then think of the opposite of these impediments. In Chapter 5, we listed things that block our creativity, such as fears and misconceptions. What can we learn by looking at the opposite of blocks? Here are some ways of enhancing creativity using what I call creativity energizers or stimulators:

1. Necessity. "Necessity is the mother of invention." Invest some money in your project. Then you'll really need to finish it and sell it.

2. Demands, goals and time pressures are definite energizers. Set goals for yourself and put time limits on them. Tell a group of people or an important person that you will finish your project by a specific date.

3. Speed. Sometimes speed itself helps loosen up the ideas lying dormant in your subconscious mind. When it is safe to do so, force yourself to work fast. Write nonstop for five minutes without taking your pencil off the paper. Say things

off the top of your head. Don't censor.

4. Fear. Feel the fear and anxiety and go ahead anyway. Take a chance. Be bold. Let fear be your signal to be courageous and bold.

EXERCISES

This chapter consisted of many practical tools for creativity enhancement. I gave examples of these tools and prompted you with questions relating to their use. Read over this chapter and answer some of these questions if you haven't done so already.

In addition, I gave you some exercises to practice using these tools. Make sure you do these exercises and stretch your creativity muscles. Specifically, get into the habit of making "to do" lists, sketching out ideas and doing some radial outlines.

Here are some additional exercises:

★ 1. Look at a familiar picture. Clear your mind of all preconceptions and look at it with "beginner's mind." Become absorbed in the picture and lose yourself in it.

★ 2. Find three ways to change your perspective on reality. Talk to a homeless person or someone much younger or older than you. Spend some time with a person from another race or culture.

★ 3. Change levels of abstraction or geographical perspectives. For example, how would someone 100 years from now evaluate your life? How would you see your family if you lived on the moon and they were on earth?

★ 4. Take a complex problem and divide it into smaller components.

★ 5. Practice attribute listing. Use the example given in this chapter to improve on the manufacturing and design of a bicycle.

★ 6. Play around with opposites. Think up three new creativity energizers to add to the list given at the end of this chapter.

CHAPTER 10

MORE TOOLS FOR YOUR TOOLBOX

Being creative means combining knowledge and imagination.
Vincent Ryan Ruggiero,
The Art of Thinking

CHUNKS, HEURISTICS AND PATTERNS

Creativity researchers have found that experts solve problems more easily and efficiently by grouping large amounts of information into chunks. Chunks are groupings of information with common features or a grouping of problems with similar solutions. The expert can access a large data base and quickly retrieve information by scanning these chunks. Chunking also makes it easier to store new information.

Here's an example of using chunks to improve memory. Look at the numbers below.

$$149162536496481100$$

Can you memorize them in one minute? Ten minutes? Now see how much easier it is to memorize them if we chunk them into this set of numbers:

$$1^2 \quad 2^2 \quad 3^2 \quad 4^2 \quad 5^2 \quad 6^2 \quad 7^2 \quad 8^2 \quad 9^2 \quad 10^2$$

When looking for a solution, look through your data base and find a previous solution to a similar problem. Then look for patterns in your work that can help you store and retrieve solutions.

Heuristics or rules of thumb are ways of organizing information into patterns as well. They help us find solutions quickly by cutting down the time required to scan the data base. For example, your grandmother was using a rule of thumb when she diagnosed a cold after observing that you had a fever and a runny nose. This called for another rule of thumb: "Have cold, give chicken soup." What is your rule of thumb for a cold?

Here are a couple of interesting heuristics from Tom Parker's compilation entitled *Rules of Thumb.*

> *When setting up an aquarium, provide at least one gallon of water for each inch of fish.*
> **Jeff Burman, business consultant**

> *About one fifth the cost of producing a book is the cost of the paper.*
> **Marshall Lee, bookmaker**

> *One acre will park a hundred cars.*
> **E. Mankin, journalist**

Here's a rule of thumb about financial investments that I find both handy and fascinating:

To calculate how long it will take to double your money in an investment, divide 72 by the rate of return. The result is the number of years it takes to double your investment. For example, if the interest rate on a certificate of deposit is 10 percent, you will double your money in 7.2 years ($72 \div 10 = 7.2$).

Patterns help us organize information and also provide us direct clues for creative solutions. One type of pattern that I have found useful in writing is *sequencing.* A sequence is the order in which one thing follows another. Typically, narrations develop from the simple to the complex, building to a climax. Time is also an excellent element around which to build a sequence. In a song, for example, the first verse might take place yesterday, the second verse today, and the third verse tomorrow. A third type of sequence might entail physical closeness: "I see you, I touch you, I kiss you."

Trends are another form of sequence. Trends give us an indication of the general tendency, course or direction of events. Look for trends in your industry. These will provide you with excellent clues about what will be successful tomorrow. Look for trends in your junk mail or in newspaper advertisements. Listen to the radio for trends in popular music. For example, synthesizers were very popular in the eighties, but the nineties have seen a trend away from techno music and back to acoustic music. Everybody seems to be recording "unplugged" albums! Browse your bookstore. What are the new themes? What will be the new titles in the coming era of electronic publishing?

ANALOGIES

A fundamental process in successful problem-solving is the ability to relate our current problems to previous ones that have already been solved. This process is the cornerstone of what Swiss psychologist Piaget calls assimilation and accommodation. As we take in or assimilate the external world, we change it. We apply our successful problem-solving strategies and solutions. At the same time, the external world changes us. We accommodate our strategies to fit each new situation. Thus, we don't reinvent the wheel every time. The more similar our new problems are to the old ones, the easier it is to apply previous coping and creativity strategies.

When we compare two things and discover their similarity or partial resemblance, we are making an analogy. Analogies are ways of transferring solutions from one problem area to another. Buying a house is analogous to buying a car, so we could take the skills learned from the latter to apply to the former. Similarly, writing an essay or short story is analogous to writing a letter.

One type of analogy is the simile. We use similes when we make direct comparisons and say "this is like this." What might we learn about someone who says "I felt as light as a feather"?

Think about these other similes:
Managing a company is like running a family.
My project is like cooking a meal.
The mind is like a computer.
A family is like the solar system.

A metaphor is a comparison that leaves out the words "like" or "as" in making the connection. For example, we are using a metaphor when we say "life is a bowl of cherries." "Love is a battlefield" portrays a much different perspective than "love is a rose." Consider these other metaphors:

All the world's a stage.
I am the sun. You are the moon.
This product is a magnet.

Solve some of your problems using metaphors and similes and other analogies. For example, if love is a rose, then what are its good qualities and what are its bad qualities?

If your company is like a football team:

■ Who is the quarterback?

■ In what quarter of the game are you?

■ Do you need to punt in order to avoid being backed into a corner?

■ Who are the referees?

If your team is like a musical group:

■ Who is the bass player and who is the drummer?

■ Are you in harmony?

■ What would happen if you played in a different key?

■ Is dissonance necessarily bad?

■ Who's the best improvisor?

How does your view of your company change when you think of it as a family rather than a military unit?

Nature is a good source for metaphorical thinking. Thomas Edison was inspired to branch out from main ideas to related ideas. He loved to look at nature because "nature doesn't just makes leaves; it makes branches and trees and roots to go with them." Thus, Edison always pursued the tree of knowledge, planted idea seeds, and sought out the root causes of things.

Some metaphors become aphorisms. Aphorisms are sayings that offer some universal truth or wisdom such as "the early bird gets the worm," and "a stitch in time saves nine."

Making analogies between one area of knowledge and another can lead to innovative developments. Did you know that football helmets were improved by making them analogous to the heads of woodpeckers? It's true. A woodpecker receives constant jolts to the head because of his natural inclination to peck wood. Researchers asked: "Why doesn't he get a concussion?" They examined the woodpecker and found dense spongy bones, tightly packed in a narrow brain, with very little fluid to transmit shock and encircled by shock-absorbing muscles. As a result of this analogy, football helmets were improved by using a lighter, thicker, strong but spongy material with a thin, hard outer shell.

Be careful not to take the analogy too far, however. There are pitfalls. One danger is that we might overly prejudice our thinking by using previously successful solutions. In a sense, this technique is the opposite of beginner's mind. Superficial analogies are another danger. They can lead to unsound reasoning. Political scientist Yuen Foong Khong of Harvard University says that U.S. policy makers erred in Vietnam because they thought it was analogous to the Korean War. Although there were similarities, there were also big differences. By taking the analogy too far, many of these differences were ignored—with disastrous results.

COMBINATIONS

Many inventions have come about by combining previously unrelated items. A Band-Aid is a combination of gauze pad and surgical tape. The printing press came about when Gutenberg combined a grape press and a coin press. A Ziploc bag combines the idea of a zipper with plastic. A sofa bed is the combination of a sofa and a bed. A camper is a synthesis of a car and a home. A clock radio is the synthesis of a clock and a radio.

Combine two items into a new idea. A fun way of doing this exercise is to pick any two items at random and combine them. You could pick the names of the items out of a newspaper, from a TV show, off a bookshelf or wherever. One of my favorite sources is the dictionary.

Here's a game you can play. Make two columns on a sheet of paper. Open your dictionary to any place at random and select a word. Place it in column one. Open it again and select another word. Place it in column two. Do this until you have five or six words in each column. Your columns might look like this.

college	crow
religion	tuition
fly	nail
puppet	soft
translate	grill

Now connect the words in column one with those in column two. Make as many connections as you like.

Combining opposites is a similar method of coming up with fresh ideas. Albert Rothenberg, in *The Emerging Goddess,* explores this method in detail and reports his findings from interviews with Nobel prize, Pulitzer prize and National Book Award winners. These creators used "Janusian thinking," a technique named after the Roman god Janus, who had two faces looking in opposite directions. Accordingly, Janusian thinking "entails actively conceiving of two or more opposite or antithetical ideas, images, or concepts simultaneously." The son of Nobel laureate Niels Bohr reportedly said his father's favorite saying was that there are "two sorts of truths, profound truths recognized by the fact that the opposite is also a profound truth, in contrast to trivialities where opposites are obviously absurd."

HYPOTHETICAL SCENARIOS

Formulating a hypothetical scenario is especially popular in science and in the court room. It is related to the previous technique of attribute listing. We simply ask: "What if?"

What if people had two heads?

What if we were visited by creatures 10,000 years more evolved than humans?

What if you had three wishes?

What if you looked extremely gorgeous or handsome?

What if you had been a prodigy?

What if I were reborn as a. . . .

A related technique is to take a situation and think of the worst thing and the best thing that could happen. Then lessen the worst and strengthen the best.

VARIATIONS ON A THEME

Review the second phase of the technique called attribute listing which was described earlier. Take the attributes game and use it to make variations on existing products or ideas. Modify, substitute, combine, adapt, magnify, minimize or rearrange the attributes.

LETTING GO

Make absurd or unusual associations. This type of thinking pushes the situation to the limits. Swami Beyondananda calls this process absurdiveness training. Push the logical mind to the limits. Turn things around in bizarre and unusual associations and combinations.

Don't be afraid to think the impossible. Reach for the stars. Be Bill Gates for an hour. Exaggerate. Win an Oscar. See a car larger than a bus. Think of a house as big as a hotel.

Thinking big will prevent you from getting lost in the woods. It will help you see the forest as well as the trees. Thinking small will let you pay attention to details and fine-tune your work. It will keep you from missing important pieces of the puzzle.

SERENDIPITY

Be on the lookout for unusual or out of the ordinary happenings. Very often we stumble into a new solution accidentally. However, it is only the prepared mind that is able to take this accident and turn it into a discovery. Invariably, when I am looking for one word in my thesaurus, I stumble into another word that is even more precise.

Nitrocellulose, a substitute for gunpowder, was discovered by serendipity. The inventor, C. F. Schonbein, accidentally spilled some nitric acid in his kitchen and quickly wiped it up with an apron. While hanging over the stove to dry, the apron burst into flames. This led Schonbein to further experiments and, eventually, to the discovery of nitrocellulose.

While conducting a series of experiments using cathode ray tubes, W. C. Roentgen discovered the X ray. He had left out some paper covered with the chemical barium platinocyanide, which had been used in another experiment. To his surprise, the paper glowed whenever he turned on the cathode ray tube. His discovery of the X ray was not far behind.

Other serendipitous discoveries include Watt inventing the steam engine after noticing steam screaming from a teapot, and Newton formulating the law of gravity after being hit by an apple falling from a tree.

But beware. If you are not looking for new discoveries, you will overlook them. In his essay "On the Part Played by Accident in Invention and Discovery," physicist Ernst Mach wrote that many accidental events "were seen numbers of times before they were noticed."

Chance favors the prepared mind.
Louis Pasteur

LOOKING AT THINGS BACKWARD

Another technique that makes use of opposites is reverse thinking or looking at things backwards. Here are some examples:

1. Take the following statement: "My recordings don't sound as good as records I hear on the radio." Now change this statement into a negative: "Not all my recordings don't sound as good as records on the radio." This would mean that some of my recordings do sound as good as records on the radio. This in turn could lead us to examine these other recordings to see how they are different.

2. In addition to defining what your problem is, define what your problem is not. In the above example, the poor recording is not about my playing technique. It is not about the quality of the instrument played or the quality of the recording equipment. So maybe it's about the specific recording techniques used. If so, then I would begin to examine my microphone placement, use of reverb, equalization, etc.

3. Figure out what everybody else doesn't do. What do competitors not do? Continuing with our example, maybe they don't use a particular style of playing that emphasizes arpeggios or exotic rhythms. Also, we might notice that the competition is not marketing their products in certain communities.

4. What if . . . . What if I stretch it, enlarge it, soften it or thicken it? Use any verb from the dictionary. This might lead me to get closer to the microphone or use more reverb or boost up certain frequencies of the sound spectrum.

5. Change directions or location. Listen to the recording from different vantage points in the studio. In addition, listen to it on different speakers. Often a recording will sound very different on a car stereo than on a home stereo.

6. Flip-flop results: "How can I produce a terrible recording?" This is the use of opposites discussed earlier. Remember

"1001 Ways to Make Yourself Miserable?" Turn defeat into victory or victory into defeat.

Here's another possible way of using the backwards technique. I touched on this earlier when I suggested that you visualize your project completed when you are in the first stage of creativity. Now visualize your problem as already solved. Experience the feeling and state of mind you are in. Look carefully at the solution. Now step backwards to a point just before your project was completed or your problem solved. Keep doing this until you have the entire solution visualized.

SYNECTICS

Synectics is a method developed by William J. J. Gordon for defining problems in a way that "makes the strange, familiar" and the "familiar, strange." There are four different types of analogies that can be used to join different and apparently irrelevant elements.

Personal analogy is very similar to "groking," which we discussed earlier in this chapter. Imagine yourself to be the object you are working on. For example, you could ask yourself, "What would it feel like if I were a table or a hammer?"

In direct analogy you discover a similarity between two different objects or processes. How are a paintbrush and a vacuum cleaner similar? What do a baseball team and a business enterprise have in common?

Symbolic analogy uses symbols, such as mathematical symbols, stories or myths, to describe a problem. The myth of Beauty and the Beast is a good analogy for analyzing some modern relationships. The beautiful person sees beyond the superficial appearance of the beast and sees the internal beauty. The beast is also endowed with instinctual powers that are lacking in the beauty and to which she is attracted in the beast.

Fantasy analogy requires the suspension of logic and reality to formulate wild ideas. Earlier we used this in creating ideal solutions and in the technique of thinking big. Imagining yourself becoming an antivirus traveling through the human body looking for viruses may be an example of fantasy analogy.

BRAINSTORMING

Brainstorming was developed by Alex Osborne to enhance group creativity, but it can be used effectively alone or with one other person. We briefly encountered brainstorming in Chapter 9 in the discussion of radial outlining. Brainstorming is a technique of letting your thoughts flow out freely to come up with new and varied ideas.

Here are four basic rules that I recommend when brainstorming:

1. Quantity leads to quality. You want to allow for the expression of as many ideas, thoughts or images as possible. Do not let the inner critic inhibit you. Do not censor or edit at this point. This is true whether you are brainstorming in the preparation stage or in the illumination stage. The more ideas you produce, the higher the probability that one of them will be a winner.

A fitting analogy in this regard is in the story of the pearl diver. Imagine a pearl diver in his boat going into the ocean to dive for pearls. Looking for the precious gems, the pearl diver gets to a place where he believes he will find many oysters. He dives deep into the water and brings up one oyster and puts it in the boat. He then opens the shell to see if there is a pearl inside. When he doesn't find one, he dives in again for another oyster. He repeats this process over and over until, finally, he finds a pearl.

Obviously this method of pearl diving is very slow and unproductive. Had the diver brought up bunches of oysters with each dive and kept going until he had large quantities in the boat, he could have opened hundreds of oysters at one sitting. In this manner, he would gather many more oysters in less time, with less effort, and increase his chances of success. Don't be like the diver in this story when you problem-solve. Dive in, bring up as many ideas as you can and keep on diving. After you've gathered a large quantity, examine and refine your ideas.

We are brainstorming. At some point, however, we will change the number of ideas by just one more and we will experience a qualitative change. So don't be discouraged when you don't readily see qualitative differences. Think of it as heating water to the boiling point.

2.   Have fun. Allow yourself to do whatever you feel like doing. Be ridiculous, silly, absurd and spontaneous. Do not doubt yourself. Let go!

3.   Free associate. Let things that might come together, come together, no matter how absurd or silly they seem.

4.   Suspend judgment. Don't put yourself down and don't put your partner or collaborator down. Do not censor!

LATERAL THINKING

Puzzles are mind-stretching exercises. Crossword puzzles, for example, stretch our vocabulary and force us to search our memory banks for facts. When our memory comes up short, we run to the dictionary or thesaurus for answers. In so doing, we increase our vocabulary and verbal knowledge.

Lateral thinking puzzles are fun, entertaining and provide a good antidote for lazy and rigid thinking. They are like crossword puzzles except they force us to think sideways. If we take a direct, straight approach, they are unsolvable. Here are a couple of puzzles from Sloane and MacHale's books *Great Lateral Thinking Puzzles* and *Challenging Lateral Thinking Puzzles:* (Answers are at the end of this chapter.)

1.   If removing an appendix is called an appendectomy and removing tonsils is called a tonsillectomy, what do we call removing a growth from your head?

2.   Do they have a 4th of July in England?

3.   Look at the diagram below. Connect all nine dots by making *only four* lines without taking your pencil off the paper.

O   O   O

O   O   O

O   O   O

4. Add one line to the following figure to make a six.

IX

EXERCISES

1. Write down three examples of information you have grouped into chunks. Think of an area where you have lots of information and where you have some expertise.

2. Write down some rules of thumb. Do you have a rule of thumb when shopping for groceries or a car? How about a rule of thumb for how much TV you will watch on week nights? Think up as many as you can.

3. What is the most important trend in the growth of your industry? Do your future plans take into account such trends as the aging of America? Have you computerized your business? Write down three more trends that are important to consider in your line of work.

4. Earlier in this chapter, we compared a family to the solar system and a team to a band of musicians. What analogy can you use to compare to your family or to your job?

5. Complete the following sentence using metaphorical language:

    A. Life is . . .

    B. My mind is . . .

    C. Love is . . .

    D. Creativity is . . .

6. Make two columns of words on a sheet of paper. Connect them in any way you like. Write a one-page story about each combination.

Answers to Lateral Thinking Puzzles:

  1. A haircut

  2. Yes

  3.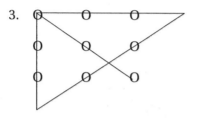

  4. SIX

CHAPTER 11

CHANGING LANGUAGES

⚜

. . . this new language, when integrated with the language of verbal, analytic thought, may provide the ingredients essential not only for true creativity—that is, new or novel ideas, insights, inventions, or discoveries that have social value—but also for useful creative solutions to the problems of everyday life.

**Betty Edwards, *Drawing on
the Right Side of the Brain***

Drawing, dancing, and music are nonverbal languages that can help us gain fresh perspectives on reality. They can shake us up from our habitual ways of knowing and experiencing the world around us. Dreaming and humor are additional methods of accessing unconscious creative material and capturing fresh insights. As methods of creativity enhancement, the strategies discussed in this chapter use several of the techniques and tools described in the previous two chapters.

To be shaken out of the ruts of ordinary perception, to be shown for a few timeless hours the outer and the inner world, not as they appear to an animal obsessed with words and notions, but as they are apprehended, directly and unconditionally, by Mind at large—this is an experience of inestimable value to everyone.

Aldous Huxley

DANCING

Dancing reflects our relationship to the world. It is an expression of our personality and style of creativity. Dance is a way of communicating and expressing our longings and values. It is a language just as verbal communications are a language. It can be useful to relieve stress, shake out our inhibitions, loosen up the subconscious and bring up new material to consciousness.

In *Creating an Imaginative Life,* musician Michael Jones writes of his experience accompanying dancers and how it helped expand his creativity. Michael was hired to play piano for a dance class. When the instructor asked him to play some music with "rain" in it, he was dumbfounded. He had never played "rain" on the piano. Eventually, he began to play "a small cluster of notes quickly and lightly on the upper keys." He was then asked to play "wind." After watching the "grand sweeping motion" of the dancers' arms, he began imitating a similar body movement on the keyboard. He was playing "wind"and it felt like "wind." Similarly, when asked to play "thunder and lightning," he watched the whirling movement on the dance floor and began playing "bass notes, creating jagged, dissonant chords up and down the keyboard." Soon he was playing "trees" and opening new doors of musical improvisations. Watching dancers and imitating their movements released his imagination. This is also an excellent technique for sculptors, painters, interior designers, actors and other performers.

Dance is both a good stress reliever and an idea releaser. It is also a good analogy for the creative process itself. After all, the Buddhists say the creative activity of the Cosmos is the dance of the God Shiva.

Here are some interesting questions to consider:

1. In what way is your work like a dance?

2. In what ways are the workings of a company like a dance?

3. How are marriage and dancing alike?

4. What does it mean to waltz your way through life?

5. When you leave a meeting, who do you usually boogie with?

6.   Do you dance around your problems?

7.   Why does it take two to tango?

8.   Have you ever been spun around?

Dance and release feelings, images and ideas from your body. Let yourself go with your kinesthetic senses and the impulses of your instincts. You don't need to go to a dance hall or club to dance. Do it wherever you have a little privacy. Don't call it dancing. Call it moving and swaying. Let your body express your inner feelings. Do it by yourself or grab a partner. Play some music or dance to the sounds inside your head. Clap your hands. Grab a prop (a scarf, a broom, a musical instrument). Express whatever emotion you are feeling at the moment. Release your soul from anger, pain and grief. Let your spirits soar with joy and passion.

DRAWING

*How can one learn the truth by thinking? As one learns to
see a face better if one draws it.*
Ludwig Wittgenstein, philosopher

Drawing is another marvelous way of unblocking creativity and a proven method for fleshing out ideas. As Betty Edwards says in her books, *Drawing on the Artist Within* and *Drawing on the Right Side of the Brain,* drawing can change our perceptions of reality and give us a new way of seeing.

*Your images are unique and important and belong to the
world, for you know something the world needs. The
knowledge that comes through your images cannot arrive
in any other way.*
Pat Allen in *Art is a Way of Knowing*

Like dancing, drawing is a language system and a way of knowing. It is a nonlinear (or right brain) mode of perception. One of Betty Edwards's most dramatic techniques is to draw a portrait by looking at it upside down. Try it. The results are quite amazing. By looking at the portrait upside down, we bypass our logical and our habitual ways of perceiving. In a sense, we look at the portrait with a beginner's mind. We see the lines and forms of the portrait as they are rather than through our preconceived ideas and labels. A face is not a face, but a series of lines and shapes. A related technique is to draw the background shapes (negative space) instead of an object. The focus is on the ground rather than on the figure. Again, in order to draw in this way, we must see with fresh eyes and suspend our logical minds. A third technique is to draw with our nondominant hand. By so doing, we access the nondominant side of our brain.

Here are several ways drawing can be used creatively:

1. Doodling. Just put marks down on the paper. Let your emotions express themselves spontaneously. Do this with your nondominant hand. Don't judge your results.

2. Draw your emotions. Take an emotion such as fear or anger and draw it. Add color with crayons and textures with shadings.

3. Draw your blocks and creativity obstacles. Draw your inner critic. Then burn these drawings!

4. Draw your creativity stimulators and enhancers. Pin up these drawings in your work space.

5. Make a drawing of your project both as it is now and as you would like to see it ideally completed. Color it in the colors that express the emotional tone of your project at present.

MUSIC

Just as dancing and drawing stimulate our right brain processes, music creates new spaces and changes our sense of time from linear to nonlinear. Our everyday language indicates that, even outside the sphere of music, we tend to think in musical terms.

Consider the following phrases:

1. They're not in harmony with each other.

2.   He marches to a different drummer.

3.   Get into the rhythm of things.

4.   You're out of tune from the rest of us.

5.   We need to fine-tune this product.

6.   It just doesn't sound right.

7.   If you don't have all the tools, improvise.

If you play a musical instrument, you know the benefits of music in reducing stress and releasing pent-up emotions. Consider improvising and letting yourself create new spaces and sounds on your instrument. Imitate wind or rain. Visualize a lake or a forest while you play. Visualize your block or a present obstacle. Let your emotions be your guides.

If you don't play an instrument, do these same exercises to stimulate your right brain while listening to music. Sit quietly in a room without distractions and listen to your favorite music. Become aware of the spaces between the notes. Pick out one instrument at a time and listen closely to what that instrument is doing. Do this with every instrument on the recording. Now try this same process with different, preferably unfamiliar recordings.

After you have heard each instrument individually, listen to them in groups and see how they interact. Music is communication. Enjoy the conversations between various instruments. Listen to the whole composition. Follow the story from beginning to end. As a story, it begins simply, builds to a climax and then comes to a definite conclusion or fades away.

As you listen to the music, become absorbed in the music and lose yourself in it. Let your mind disappear.

Pick up any musical instrument and play music even if you aren't proficient at it. Play a simple instrument like a maraca or a cow bell. Almost anything can be a percussion instrument on which you can play rhythm. Try several of them at once. Play along with a piece of music you like.

Take a melody instrument and play single notes. Make up a melody. Start with two notes and play them in different rhythmic patterns. Remember the song "One Note Samba?" Multiple sections of the original song are composed entirely of a single note! The song changes sections and then goes on for a considerable length on another single note! Carlos Jobim, the famous and brilliant Brazilian composer, added a bridge and the song became an international hit.

Related to music is poetry and songwriting. Writing a poem or a song is an excellent way of getting in touch with emotions that are otherwise difficult to express. Write a rap song that expresses where you are right now in your creative project.

HUMOR

Laughter is the best medicine to help keep us physically and mentally healthy. It also promotes creativity. Laughter jolts us out of our habitual patterns and gives us a new perspective on reality. Through the use of irony, exaggeration, word play and absurd associations, it surprises us and keeps us on our toes. Laughter shakes up our physical system and rearranges our thoughts.

A film about the writer/philosopher Alan Watts made a lasting impression on me many years ago. Mr. Watts, author of numerous books on Zen and Hindu philosophy, demonstrated the technique of "laughter yoga." He worked himself up from a calm meditative state to a condition in which he was shaking and roaring with laughter. He started with simple grunts to activate his belly. He then increased the movement of his belly and the volume of the laughter coming out of his mouth. Within a short time he was roaring with laughter and his body was shaking all over. He could make himself laugh at will. What a great technique! I've used it many times since then (during very private moments, of course) and it works. It's a sure way of getting rid of stress and changing your mood.

Humor also provides perspective and frees us from narrow thinking. Allen Klein tells us in *The Healing Power of Humor,* "It is not so much the actual event that causes us pain as how we relate to it." He tells us a humorous story about a college coed's letter to her mom and dad. Here's the letter:

Dear Mom and Dad.

I am sorry that I have not written, but all my stationery was destroyed when the dorm burned down. I am now out of the hospital and the doctor said that I will be fully recovered soon. I have also moved in with the boy who rescued me, since most of my things were destroyed in the fire.

Oh yes, I know that you have always wanted a grand-child, so you will be pleased to know that I am pregnant and you will have one soon.

Love,
Mary

P.S. There was no fire, my health is perfectly fine, and I am not pregnant. In fact, I do not even have a boyfriend.

However, I did get a D in French and a C in math and chemistry, and I just wanted to make sure that you keep it all in perspective.

This "joke" is a variation of the "bad news/good news" formula that Johnny Carson used so effectively. Swami Beyondananda, the master of word play, also uses the formula in his message to all who search for Ultimate Truth. He says, "I hate to tell you this, boychick, but there is no key to the Universe. That's the bad news. The good news is, it's been left unlocked."

The Swami also tells us that he dyed his hair multicolored to open up his "clown chakra." In another pearl of wisdom regarding self-criticism and fear of failure, the Swami suggests turning state-ments like "I'm a failure" into "I am tremendously successful at failing." For dealing with blocks, he writes, "If you feel blocked, ask your inner child for help. Your inner child loves to play with blocks!" In regard to procrastination he says, "Next time you get the urge to procrastinate, put it off." If you want more of these gems, read the Swami's *Driving Your Own Karma* or *When You See a Sacred Cow, Milk It For All It's Worth.*

Humor frees us from the constraints of rational thought and, not surprisingly, research studies have linked humor and creativity.

After listening to a recording by a popular comedian, students scored higher on tests of fluency, flexibility and originality.

Jokes help us keep our perspective. Next time you're feeling down about your age, remember, "It's better to be over the hill than under it."

Allen Klein recommends that we put cutouts of laughing lips, smile buttons and clown cards on our bulletin board. He also suggests going to toy stores, garage sales and secondhand stores to find inexpensive laugh reminders. Try it for yourself. Clip out humorous material from newspapers and magazines and post them in your workplace.

Here are a few other suggestions, inspired by Klein's and Swami's books, that could prove very useful in problem-solving.

1. If nobody listens to you because there's too much noise, try mouthing without making a sound. This should grab people's attention.

2. If you are suffering from stage fright, visualize the audience nude or as tiny, cute animals.

3. In the middle of an argument with a friend who is intent on not listening, grab a napkin, or whatever prop is available, and pretend you are using a microphone. You might start your announcement by saying, "now hear this, now hear this."

4. Get up on the side of the bed opposite what you are used to. Eat your breakfast with your non-dominant hand, walk backwards around the house or tell everybody it's your birthday when it isn't.

5. Open up your clown chakra. Get some help from one of your imaginary allies. How about the Swami himself? When you feel weighted down, ask him to show you how to lighten up. Whenever you are caught in a difficult and tense situation, ask your clown for a humorous solution.

Remember that creative ideas often come when we are just "fooling around," "clowning around" or "playing with old ideas."

DREAM PROGRAMMING

Dreams have their own language and reveal the workings of the subconscious mind. The interpretation of dreams has always been a subject of fascination for scholars, philosophers, artists and scientists. Today, many people are exploring the dream world on a daily basis. Understanding the language of your dreams releases creative energy and improves the quality of your life.

Research shows that all human beings dream every night. Although you may not remember your dreams the next morning, you usually have several dreams during a typical night's sleep. And dreams serve an important function. Research has shown that when a person is deprived of sleeping and dreaming, he begins to hallucinate. Hallucinations, in these cases, are nothing more than dreaming while awake. Dreams have also been described as stress releasers. In his book, *Where People Fly and Water Runs Uphill*, Jeremy Taylor offers ten basic assumptions about dreams, based upon 20 years of dream research. He concludes that "all dreams reflect inborn creativity and ability to face and solve life's problems."

Great discoveries have been made as a result of dreams. Elias Howe, who invented the lock stitch sewing machine, found the solution to his problem in a nightmare. He had reached an impasse in his work. He couldn't get the machine needle to bob up and down without getting the thread all tangled up. One night he dreamed he was being boiled alive by cannibals with spears. Keen observer that he was, Howe noticed that the spears had holes in the tips. He was consciously looking for a solution to his problem, and "Eureka," his dream gave him the answer. Rather than threading the machine needle in the middle, as conventional machines did, Howe realized that the solution was to thread the needle at the tip, just like the spears that the cannibals used!

Here's another example of creative inspiration in a dream. August Kekule, a chemistry professor, dreamed of large structures that were "twining and twisting in snake-like motion." He was then startled and saw that "One of the snakes had seized hold of its own tail, and the form whirled mockingly before my eyes. As if by a flash of lightning I awoke." Kekule's dream led him to revolutionize organic chemistry by formulating the molecular structure of the benzene ring.

Everyday problem-solving can also be a result of a dream, as in this story by Jeff Yip. In an article in the *Los Angeles Times* (July 3, 1995), Jeff humorously states that real information is not in the Internet but in the "inner net." He tells the story of Dan Gold, a plumbing fixtures executive with Price Pfister, who was stumped in working on a new motor/gizmo. The final words of a dream were: "What you're looking for is in Kansas." When he woke up, Gold did not know what the dream meant. He had never been to Kansas. After spending some time perplexed about the dream, he made a phone call to a friend in Kansas and asked him to look in the local business-to-business phone book under *motors*. Gold then called the only listing and found the exact part he was looking for to complete his gizmo.

In order to tap the wisdom of your subconscious mind, you must first of all begin to pay attention to your dreams. You must give them validity and importance. Expect to remember your dreams and to find answers to your questions in your dreams. Imagine yourself remembering and recording your dreams. Trust the wisdom of dreams.

Then begin writing down your dreams. Keep paper and pencil handy by your bedside so you can record your dreams or fragments of them immediately upon awakening. Learn to write key phrases and describe vivid images in the dark so that you can reconstruct your dream in the morning. You might find that a voice-activated tape recorder works better for you. Whatever method you use, always stay as close to the images and feelings of the actual dream as you can. Upon awakening in the morning, write out the dream fragments in greater detail or record the dream anew.

Once you have mastered this part of the process, you could read Patricia Garfield's book *Creative Dreaming* or Carlos Castaneda's books. Dr. Garfield shows us how to plan and control our dreams. Don Juan, Carlos Castaneda's mentor, also has a lot to say about dreams and their ability to transform our lives. Both Patricia Garfield and Don Juan recommend learning how to experience the vivid dream before attempting to manipulate the dream.

EXERCISES

★ 1. Do some "laughter yoga." Start with the syllable HA and say it three or four times in succession. Use your diaphragm and make your belly move out and in as you say HA, HA, HA. Next, do the same thing using the syllable HE. Then add HO. Finally put all three together and work yourself up to a roaring belly laugh. Do this exercise while recalling a funny event in your life.

★ 2. Put on your favorite music and dance. Be free with your body. Don't think about what you're doing. Just go with your feelings. Become absorbed in the music and let your body dictate where it wants to go.

★ 3. After you have done the exercise described in #2, use metaphors and analogies to guide your movements. Dance like the wind or like thunder. Be a bird or a tiger.

★ 4. Look over the exercises suggested under the heading Drawing. Do any you have not already done. Invent some new ones.

★ 5. If you play a musical instrument, try some of the improvising tips suggested in this chapter. Play "wind" or "rain." Take different emotions and play them. For example, play "jealousy" or "rage."

★ 6. Play a musical portrait. For fun, have a friend or loved one sit for you while you "paint" a musical portrait of them. Focus on them while playing your instrument. Can you get to the core of their personality and express it in your music?

★ 7. Make up a melody that describes how you feel right now. Be aware of the mood of the melody as reflected in the rhythm and the brightness or darkness of it. Next, write some words to your melody.

★ 8. Think of some unpleasant situation you have been in lately. Perhaps it involves a problem with a friend, boss, employee or loved one. How could you have used humor to turn the situation into a pleasant one?

★ 9. Write down the first dream that comes into your mind. Take each element of the dream and talk with it. An element can be a person, place, thing, mood or anything you can identify as a part of the whole. Become the element. "Grok" it (see Chapter 9). Make friends with the scary parts. Ask each part to reveal its meaning to you.

★ 10. Rate yourself on how much you value verbal communication over non-verbal communication. What are the advantages of each for you?

★ 11. Sit with a friend and communicate non-word sounds (grunts and nonsense syllables) for 10 minutes.

PART FOUR

BREAKTHROUGH TO FINAL TRANSFORMATION

At any age, we can challenge and conquer the last false assumption and touch the incandescent stream within us that causes a light of meaning to shine on our life from inside out.

Roger L. Gould, M.D.,
Transformations

CHAPTER 12

FINE-TUNING

The difference between the right word and the almost right
word is the difference between lightning and the lightning bug.
Mark Twain

All right. You've captured lightning in a bottle. Now you'll top it off and make your work shine brilliantly through the process of fine-tuning your product. This is the time for polishing and refining. Put on the Judge's robe and be critical and judgmental. Be tough but fair to yourself.

In this chapter we will also move into a whole new realm of creative activity. You will become a salesperson preparing to take your product to market. This involves persuading others of the value of your work. In some cases, you may even have to fight to stay competitive. The Warrior role, described in Chapter 4, will become very important now.

In the process of marketing and selling your work, you will probably bounce back from criticism and possibly face rejection. Reacting defensively and negatively to criticism can make enemies out of potential allies. If you are unable to manage rejection, you risk early burn out. Learning to bounce back takes practice, emotional honesty and good humor. How you manage criticism and rejection can mean the difference between failure and success!

One thing that separates us from genius is not paying attention to and not valuing our flashes of insight. Geniuses search for answers and capture their insights on little pieces of paper, on tape recorders, on painting canvases and computer screens. Don't let your flashes get away. Recognize them as breakthroughs from normal perceptions. Give them importance. Value them.

POLISHING AND REFINING

Oh, how difficult it is to make anyone see and feel in music what we see and feel ourselves.
Pyotr Ilich Tchaikovsky

You've come a long way. You've done your research and struggled through the earlier stages of the creative process. By now you've had a few Eureka experiences. Becoming aware of and appreciating these small flashes of insight and illumination prepares the way for the larger lightning bolts ahead. Here are a few phrases that will alert you that you have caught some lightning in a bottle.

- Aha!
- That's it!
- Oh Wow!
- Far Out!
- Awesome!
- I Got It!

Perhaps you've already captured a powerful bolt of lightning and had a life-transforming experience. It's also possible that your product or idea came to you complete and in a polished state. If so, and if you intend to present your work to others, it would still be advisable to look over your work. Verify that your information is correct and up-to-date and that your logic is sound. Tighten up any loose ends before going to the marketplace.

Even if you haven't captured lightning yet, you may at least have had some light shine on your work. In many cases, that's good enough. Keep working and polishing.

If your project involves writing, now's the time for rewriting. As a serious writer, you have already read such books as *Writing Down the Bones* by Natalie Goldberg and *Getting the Words Right* by Theodore Cheney. Apply your craft to trim the fat. Eliminate the unnecessary. Leave only the essentials. Consider the whole. Don't become too attached to any part. If something needs to be thrown out for the good of the whole, do it. Often, you must part with your favorite word and phrase because it just isn't right for what you are trying to communicate.

> *I rewrote the ending to* A Farewell to Arms, *the last page of it, thirty-nine times before I was satisfied.*
> **Ernest Hemmingway**

This is the time to spell-check, use the thesaurus and check your grammar. Include variety in your sentence length and be consistent in your style. Consider whether reorganization would improve your creation. Perhaps the third paragraph should be the first. Perhaps the last verse of your song or poem should really be the second. Perhaps there is one line that is stronger than all the rest and bears repeating.

If you have been working on an event or performance, this is the time to rehearse until you have ironed out all the rough areas. Have you used visualization to practice your performance in front of an imaginary audience? Can you clearly see success in your mind's eye? Have you made a dry run to make sure you've thought of everything? Are all the details in place? Also, I recommend that you practice your routine in front of a live audience, if possible. Schedule a trial run with a small group of friends or perform in a small theater or club. Comedians, musicians and other performers do this all the time. They test their material in safe and small markets and use the feedback to improve their "products."

Playing devil's advocate is an extremely useful tool in fine-tuning your product. It allows you to anticipate your critics and disarm them. Pretend you are your worst critic. What would you criticize about your work? How would you answer your critic?

Criticism is one major benefit of testing your product in a small group. Listen carefully to the feedback you get. Don't ignore criticisms because you're challenged. Incorporate useful information to improve your product.

In this entire fine-tuning phase, a variety of tools described in earlier chapters can be used to improve your product. In addition to visualization, use attribute listing to tighten things up. List the strong and weak attributes. Strengthen different aspects of your project or eliminate the weak points. Don't be content with strengthening only one weakness. Be thorough and tough. Strengthen as many weaknesses as you can identify. Keep on looking for weaknesses until you are satisfied you've done a thorough job.

Also, don't forget to add advantages and strengths that you had previously overlooked. For example, if your product has a price advantage over other products, add ease of use and durability as advantages. This is especially important if you are thinking of taking you work to market or to your boss. Make it as good as you can make it. Add value to your work to make it more appealing and marketable. Make the components of higher quality or increase the number of features. Your customer may want more "bells and whistles."

Now look back at your initial vision. Does your final creation live up to that vision? If not, what's missing? Or what's changed?

Making a movie is like climbing a mountain. The higher you get, the more tired and breathless you become, but your view becomes much more extensive.
Ingmar Bergman

Earlier in the book, I suggested that you try out your ideas in a focus group. A focus group serves a similar purpose now. You want to discover the flaws in your product so that you have an opportunity to correct them before going to market. Now's the time to risk "failure" on a small scale and in a controlled environment. It will not be as costly in the long run. So, send out a small mailing to test the market. Put a small ad in the paper to test interest in your product. Do a survey. Build a prototype of your work for initial review.

Peer review is also very helpful in ferreting errors in thinking and clarifying crucial points. If you've been following my earlier suggestions, you have already consulted with others and possibly taken in a partner or collaborator. You have already seen your project from a perspective other than your own. Nevertheless, it's time to do it again. Before concluding your work, get additional feedback. Ask family members, send out your work for review by peers, friends or relatives. Get some professional advice if your project warrants it.

Another possibility is to join a workshop. Get together with individuals working on similar projects and critique each other's work. In Los Angeles, for example, the Songwriter's Guild of America and the National Academy of Songwriters hold workshops and seminars throughout the year where songwriters bring their material to be critiqued by the instructor and fellow students. Workshops provide an opportunity to test your materials and reveal flaws and weaknesses.

If you can't find a workshop, form your own work group. Create an environment where it is safe to bring in material that is "in progress." Ask yourself periodically, "Is there an atmosphere of trust and safety in this group?" If not, then bring this up to the group and help establish or reestablish such an atmosphere. Without it, the members will have a difficult time growing and the group will be in danger of disintegrating.

Remember the brainstorming guidelines listed in Chapter 10. Incorporate the following suggestions for developing a constructive group atmosphere:

1. Praise strengths in addition to criticizing weaknesses.

2. Be sensitive when giving feedback to others. Talk to the person's feeling as well as their intellect.

3. To make sure your criticism is constructive:

    Listen to your tone of voice both when you are giving and when you are receiving criticism. Are you being sarcastic in giving feedback? Watch out. This will injure rather than help. Are you whining when you answer your critics? This may keep people from giving you valuable feedback. In some cases, it might also get you unwarranted negative feedback. Be aware when you feel defensive or resistant to change.

4. When criticizing another's work, offer suggestions for fixing a problem or improving a product. This is constructive and shows a spirit of cooperation. It makes feedback much easier to accept.

5. Treat your fellow group members as "special." Respect their dreams.

6. Don't forget your good humor. Use it to relieve tension, but be sure it's not at the expense of a group member.

7. Practice the stress management and relaxation exercises in Chapter 7 to clear the confusion in your mind and to focus on the present needs and goals of the group members.

8. Try out one or two creativity techniques from Chapters 8, 9 and 10 each week in the group.

9. Chose one person to be group facilitator each week. The facilitator keeps the group focused on productivity and makes sure the group uses its time for maximum productivity. This person also monitors the group tone to assure that the atmosphere remains constructive.

For most of us, the creative process needs a point of completion where we truly experience our results, even if they are not what we expected and/or wanted.
William Miller

EVALUATING YOUR RISK

All this polishing, testing and refining decreases your risk when you take your work to the marketplace. The greater your investment of time, energy and money in your project, the more you need to test your product. Testing allows you to evaluate where your money, time and energy should be invested.

In evaluating your risk, ask yourself the following questions:

1. What are the consequences of my risk?

2. How much money am I risking?

3. What will I lose if I fail?

4. What will I gain if I succeed?

5. What is the worst case scenario?

6. What is the probability of failure or a bad outcome?

7. What is my risk tolerance?

8. What are the side benefits of launching my project now?

Remember that, even if you fail, the project may still be worth completing. For example, even if your project doesn't make any money directly, it may build goodwill, make new contacts for you, impress your boss, help you learn new skills, or set up a future project or business.

BOUNCING BACK FROM CRITICISM AND REJECTION

Our greatest glory is not in never failing, but in rising every time we fall.

Thomas Carlisle

So you've forged ahead with your project and gotten a good deal of feedback. No doubt some of it is negative and critical. Dealing with this type of criticism is one of the most difficult aspects of being creative. Why? Because we become attached to our creations and often take criticism too personally. We treat our creations as if they were our babies and become hurt and offended if anyone says they're ugly or unworthy of praise. If our egos are fragile, criticism can be devastating.

You can gain insight into your reaction to criticism by looking back at your childhood experiences. Children often take criticism to mean "I don't love you" or "You're not lovable." As adults, we carry over these same interpretations and feel hurt, devalued and rejected when criticized. Often we make matters worse by raising the criticism to catastrophic proportions. We add emotionally dramatic and devastating words to the critic's words. For example, the critic says, "It doesn't really fit in with our plans," and we hear, "It's not good enough." Or we exaggerate the meaning of the critic's negative words and take them to the limit. If the critic suggests that our work is not well developed, we imagine he meant "You have no talent." Then we compound the picture by adding another phrase, "Get out of this business." In the extreme, we add the *coup de grace* by convincing ourselves that behind it all, the critic really meant "You are worthless!"

> *When someone brings up a suggestion or proposes a new*
> *approach, someone else shoots it down. The process, if*
> *continued and institutionalized within the organization,*
> *will thwart creative efforts and reduce the likelihood of*
> *beneficial change.*
> **Charles "Chic" Thompson**

On the other hand, the critic can sometimes get out of line. The critic may confuse matters of personal taste with matters of fact. And rather than express a feeling of personal dislike or state that they have decided your product or creation doesn't fit with their personal needs, they declare that your work is of no value.

In cases where you're trying to please a customer, boss or contractor, their demands may become too great. You must, at times, determine whether your compromises are devaluing your work to such an extent that it demeans you. World-renowned musician Akira Tana tried to adjust his playing to please band leaders. "But," he says, "in some cases you find yourself trying to adjust so much to accommodate another performer, it gets very confusing in terms of your own musical identity. You begin to wonder, 'Well, exactly who am I?'"

The bottom line is to be open to criticism but remember this: There have been many highly successful creations that were severely criticized and rejected before they succeeded. The 1970s song "You Light Up My Life" is typical of what happens to many songs, books, screenplays and inventions. It was rejected by over one hundred publishers and producers before it became a monster hit!

One of the most common phrases you'll hear is "It won't sell!" Listen to and evaluate comments like these. Be aware that it is one person's opinion and may not be a good overall evaluation of your product. Executives, investors and bosses are often very conservative. When it comes to innovation, failure is more frequent than success. It stands to reason then, that it is safer to say no to a new product than to risk failure by saying yes.

In addition to "It won't sell," watch out for these other killer phrases:

1. It's not original enough.

2. It's *too* original.

3. It's too advanced.

4. It's outdated.

5. It's too expensive.

6. We don't do things that way.

7. People will never accept it.

8. If it's such a good idea why hasn't it already been done?

9. It's too expensive.

Here's how to put potentially destructive criticism to good use. Stay calm and don't take it personally. Learn as much as you can from your critic. Don't go away angry. See it as an opportunity to improve your product and possibly make a contact. Your worst critic could become your best ally. Build a relationship. Listen to the feedback and correct what is lacking in your work. Your critic is telling you exactly what he or she is looking for. That's very valuable information. Not only does it tell you how you might improve your product, it gives you information about other products they might be interested in. Furthermore, a critic represents more than just a single opinion. He is probably representative of other people with similar views. Use this information to anticipate future feedback.

If your critic says "It's not original" or "It won't fly" (or any such killer phrase), ask for more details. Get reasons and evidence, not just conclusions. The same applies to positive evaluations. Reasons, evidence and details are much more useful than conclusions. Don't be in a hurry to cut off communication. Ask questions such as:

1. "What was it about my product that you didn't like?"

2. "Would you be interested in . . . ?"

3. "Do you have any suggestions where I might . . . ?"

4. "What would it take to make this appealing to you?"

5. "Can you recommend anyone who would be interested in this product?"

6. "Do you have an example of the kind of thing you're looking for?"

Humor used in the right place and in the right way can be magical in winning over a critic. Paul Berliner in *Thinking in Jazz* gives us a good example of this. Jazz band leader John McNeil was trying to get his drummer to play a certain way over a melodic figure that the rest of the band was playing. The drummer, apparently, didn't like the way the whole thing sounded and refused to play his part. They argued for a while and McNeil asked the drummer for one good reason as to why he wouldn't do it. The drummer had become entrenched in his position and said, "I just think it sounds terrible and I don't like it." To this McNeil replied, "Okay, we'll compromise. Since you think it sounds terrible and you're not going to want to play it very much, we just won't do it." The ensuing laughter helped move the drummer and the whole band into a more positive direction. It also got the drummer to accept the band leader's creation that he had previously been rejecting!

Know that you have a right to be respected. Your critic can criticize your product, not you. If he is criticizing you, then he is out of line. He is not being fair and probably has an axe to grind. His criticism should be evaluated from that perspective. In other words, be aware that the intensity and tone of his criticism may be personal and biased. As one musician says, "I will accept criticism from someone I respect, but it also depends how you lay it on me." Nevertheless, something can be learned from all feedback. Detach yourself and see whether there might not be a kernel of truth buried in his bag of untruths.

Look at the bigger picture. Think like a producer, business person, entrepreneur or boss. Your project or work may just not fit into the larger project. For example, you may be a great Shakespearean actor and not fit into a comedy movie. Being rejected doesn't mean you're not a good actor. Having your product rejected doesn't mean it's not valuable. Move on and maybe come back some other time.

By being calm and objective, you will be able to evaluate the situation clearly. Before and during your interactions with the "customer," actively learn what they have to offer you. You may decide that you don't really want to be a part of this company or production. The company may be too small or offer terms that are too low or not as good as you could get elsewhere.

Some people say it is darkest just before the dawn. Don't give up. Often, rejection is a blessing in disguise. A Buddhist story tells of a man who was very disheartened when his son was passed over for military duty. He took it as a statement that his son was not good enough. His disappointment turned to relief when war broke out and many of the village sons were either killed or lost a limb in battle.

Another saying states, "If it doesn't kill you, it will make you stronger." Often when the criticism is personal, it hurts. You may have to go home and do some repair work. Learn how to deal with your anger and hurt feelings. Do some relaxation exercises and affirmations. Use visualization coupled with changing perspectives. Visualize the painful scene or the critic's words in your mind's eye. Change the distance. See the image shrink in size as it recedes into the distance. Make it disappear into the far corners of the galaxy. Separate out the information from the painful emotion. Change its intensity and importance by making it go out of focus or lose brightness. Make it spin around and explode into a million pieces!

GOING TO THE MARKETPLACE

Although this book is not about marketing, the techniques and methods described in the last few chapters will definitely help you find creative ways to market your product. Once you have finished creating your product, you are in the final stages of the creative process for that project. The final stage is the beginning of the next, however, since you are now about to launch your marketing project. And if you followed my advice regarding your initial project, you already have a great deal of material about marketing. You have already done your research and looked over the competition. You know how your product is better or different. By examining brochures, sales pitches, advertising and promotional literature— and by attending meetings and workshops—you know how competitors have promoted and marketed their products. Use those materials. Improve on them and/or modify them to fit your work.

Develop a marketing plan. If you're a large corporation, you no doubt have professionals available for this job. But if you are a small company or an individual, there are excellent marketing books available to assist you. Get a copy of Jay Conrad Levinson's book, *Guerilla Marketing*. It shows you how a small-budget company can compete with large corporations.

A marketing plan must include promotion and distribution. How will you get people to know about your product? Can you get radio and television interviews? Where can you talk to people to let them know what you have to offer? Once they decide to buy your product or service, where can they get it? Who will put it in the stores for you? As Jay Levinson states: "Marketing requires commitment, patience, confidence, and an assortment of weapons." Isn't this exactly what we have said about creativity itself? Of course it is! Successful marketing is based on the same creativity principles we have emphasized throughout this book.

CELEBRATION!

Before you actually start your marketing, though, take some time to celebrate. Savor the feeling of accomplishment. Congratulate yourself for completing your project and surviving the trials and tribulations of the journey. You have now conquered a few more of your demons.

Celebration is the last and final stage I listed in Chapter 3. If your work was a long project, hopefully you celebrated after you completed each step, because each step was a project in itself. Maybe you went out for a beer or coffee and lemon meringue pie. Some people give themselves the rest of the day off or go out for an evening of fun and entertainment. In these ways you feel the satisfaction of closure and accomplishment.

If you are like me, you enjoyed the process in itself. The journey is its own reward. Like any adventure, there are ups and downs. But your project is now complete. Take time to enjoy it and be proud of yourself for a job well done. You've just grown taller and wiser. And you've surely learned how to do it better next time.

Sometimes your project warrants throwing a celebration party. (Or maybe your project was to organize a celebration party!) Political victories are celebrated this way. So are championship games and successful harvests! Celebrations are a way of letting off steam and rewarding ourselves for the hard work we've completed. They frequently have another important purpose: to let others know about our accomplishments and to prepare the world for our next journey. Celebrate!

EXERCISES

1. Test your product before going to market. Do a survey or form a focus group. Try placing an ad in the classified section of the newspaper. See what kind of response you get.

2. Use visualizations to prepare yourself for marketing. See yourself approaching customers, stores and distributors. If

you find yourself getting anxious during these visualizations, it means you need work in these areas. Practice visualizing success.

3. Show your work to peers and ask for criticism of your work. Look for a group of individuals who are working on projects similar to yours. Either join an existing workshop or form your own group. You might start with the yellow pages of your phone book.

4. Review any recent experiences you've had with criticism. Did you overreact? Did you ask for evidence and constructive criticism? Did you get angry or did you stay calm? Did you try to make an ally out of your critic?

5. List five ways in which you have celebrated while working on your project. List five more that you could use in the future.

6. List five ways by which you can announce the completion of your project. Consider press releases, post cards, phone calls or a party.

7. Practice facing criticism and rejection. Write down various negative responses you might get to your work and answer each of these criticisms.

8. Write down four or five affirmations you can use to rebuild yourself after rejection.

Chapter 13

REACHING HIGHER GROUND

{We must} commit ourselves to the idea of nurturing our own growth. It is a lifetime process. We must learn to recognize and root out the forces that stop us from growing or lead us into dead ends. We must always remember to look first for the enemy within.

Roger L. Gould, M.D.,
Transformations

Deep within our psyches lie agreements we have made with ourselves and the world we live in. Many of these agreements were made in our childhood based on assumptions that are no longer valid. We may have agreed not to assert our point based on the assumption that we will get punished for being "uppity." We may have agreed to be "good" based on equating "goodness" with obedience and conformity.

We also harbor hurts and resentments that drain our energies and affect our ability to make commitments. We become overprotective of our deeper selves and loose touch with our greater sensibilities. Our anger and bitterness eat away at our self-confidence and distract us from our projects. We become fixated on undoing the past rather than creating our future.

Our experiences in childhood also affect our sense of trust and our faith. We ask ourselves:

- Who and how much should we trust?

- Why should we sacrifice so much for a tomorrow that may never come?

- Do we really have a higher purpose in life or is this all there is?

- To what should we commit our time and energy?"

Commitment, forgiveness and faith are outward expressions of our values and choices. They reflect the deeper levels of our psyches and are the context in which we live and create. We must examine this context to take our creative possibilities to higher ground.

COMMITMENT

Commitment in action means unfolding our potential to become bigger than the situation. Without commitment, we remain in a state of analysis—paralysis, stalemating our talent as an eternal apprentice in a world of masters.
William C. Miller

Every creation requires some degree of commitment. Commitment means surrendering part of our lives to an endeavor that may not always be enjoyable or successful. It means taking risks and investing energy. The larger the project, the more energy required to complete it, the greater our commitment must be. Completing a successful project requires sacrifice. After weeks, months or years of hard work, we may achieve our goal, only to realize it has fallen short of our ideal. We dedicate ourselves with the hope that our final product will be worth the time and effort we have committed.

Commitments are sometimes expressed publicly. When we announce that we will produce a product by a given date, we increase the likelihood that we will do so. That's because we've increased our motivation. We now have a social and, perhaps, an economic price to pay for not fulfilling our promise. We have made an agreement and must keep our part of the bargain.

Howard Gardner, in *Creating Minds*, asserts that Faustian bargains are common among creative geniuses. Faust, as you will recall, was the philosopher in Goethe's poem who sold his soul to the devil in return for knowledge and power. In his brilliant book about revolutionary geniuses of the twentieth century, Gardner states, "In general, the creators were so caught up in the pursuit of their work mission that they sacrificed all, especially the possibility of a rounded personal existence." The geniuses he is talking about are Freud, Picasso and the like. These geniuses dared not compromise their talents. "And, indeed, at times when the bargain is relaxed, there may well be negative consequence for the individual's creative output," Gardner adds.

While it may be true that many revolutionary geniuses make such Faustian bargains, little has been said of covenants with positive higher powers. The Israelites, for example, made a covenant with Jahweh (Jehovah). Among other things, they promised to make Yahweh their only god in return for protection and special treatment. Religious individuals of all persuasions also make bargains on a regular basis: vowing to do such and such in return for some special favor from God.

Almost all of us have a belief in a higher power. We may call it God, the Supreme Being, Brahman, the Transcendent Self or the Universal Force. It may not even have a name but is, nevertheless, some mysterious entity to which we turn in time of need and ask for help and support. If you actually make vows, covenants, agreements, or other commitments, make sure you honor them. These higher powers, imaginary or real, are allies that should not be betrayed or alienated.

The agreements we make with ourselves and others also affect our creative output. Sometimes these are decisions *not to do something*. These agreements, made in the distant past and long forgotten, can be holding us back today. They are often at the source of our self-destructive behavior. Children of parents who dispensed love based upon the child's performance, often engage in this type of behavior. It's as if the adult child is saying, "OK, I'll pretend to really try to succeed, but at the last minute, I'll fail. I'll make it look like it was not my own fault so that I will not be accused of not trying." Review and clarify any such agreements you may have made in the past. You may need to renegotiate in order to move forward.

Michael, a former client, was blocked by just such an agreement. As a child actor, he was cute and adorable. He had considerable success and was lavished with praise and attention. In his early twenties he was still blessed with good looks, but something was wrong. He was being passed over by producers and casting directors, and his acting career was going downhill. In therapy, he discovered the anger he felt toward his mother. He felt she only loved him for performing. Deep down he resented having to perform in order to get her love. As long as his success came easy, this was not a big problem. But now that he had to really work hard and commit energy and time to his craft, he could not muster the motivation to do so. He was holding back out of anger toward his mother. This is commonly called cutting of your nose to spite your face. To get back at his mother, he was unconsciously refusing to expend the energy needed to succeed in the acting business. However, when he was able to recapture his own pleasure in acting and reverse his decision not to give it his all, his acting career took off again.

FORGIVENESS

Hatred, rancor, and the spirit of vengeance are useless baggage to the artist. His road is difficult enough and he should cleanse his soul of everything which could make it more so.

Henri Matisse

Forgiveness is, as singer/songwriter Don Henley says, "The Heart of the Matter." To forgive is to let go of anger, bitterness and desire for revenge. Anger and bitterness are energy drains and negatively affect creative pursuits. You are much better off directing that energy onto your project. Ranting and raving about some misdeed is fine as long as it leads to constructive action to remedy the situation. In the same way, the desire for revenge is a distraction and a waste. I counsel my clients not to dwell on revenge. Revenge is like throwing good money after bad. You've already lost some valuable time and energy as a result of what you feel another person did to you. Otherwise, you wouldn't be seeking revenge. To spend more time and energy on getting back at that person is to compound the loss. Better to redirect yourself toward your goals. Free yourself of the obsession for revenge. Learn from your mistakes and move on. Let go of the negative feelings that shackle you. Revenge may even lead you to commit acts resulting in personal failure and/or serious tragedy.

> *Pain must be turned from an enemy to a potential friend,*
> *a messenger of useful information.*
> **Roger Gould, M.D.**

Here's the story of another client, Raul. He was extremely angry when he discovered that his wife and brother had an affair behind his back. The hurt was compounded by the fact that Raul had invited his brother to stay in his home while he looked for a job. Raul desperately wanted revenge. Fortunately, he learned to accept the hurt and let go of his need for revenge. Raul was very intelligent and ambitious. He needed help channeling his rage and frustration. Over time, he creatively redirected his energy toward a long-time dream of starting a printing business. His energy was put to better use in running his printing business and he avoided a potentially life-destroying tragedy.

Self-forgiveness is, in some cases, even more important than forgiving others. In our efforts toward success and perfection, we meet with a great deal of frustration. We have already seen how failure is the rule in creativity. We know that we are likely to meet with frequent rejection and hear discouraging comments along the way. If we take these comments too seriously, we may be unduly punishing ourselves. The negative voices may become internalized as our inner critic. For the most part, we have created our inner critic by internalizing the voices of our parents, teachers and friends who have directly or indirectly implanted their negativism into our subconscious mind. This voice sometimes whispers words of discouragement and clutters up our internal work space. But just as we must all learn to forgive others and not get tied up in bitterness over past events, we must be kind and generous to ourselves. We must forgive ourselves for our mistakes and limitations.

At times, you may need to let off some steam, to complain and indulge yourself in a binge of negative thinking. If you do, don't beat yourself over the head with guilt and remorse. Complain to a member of your fantasy family, your mentor, your therapist or to God. Complain, pick yourself up and move on.

FAITH

Once we begin to grasp how illusory are our uncertainties,
we can begin to enjoy our doubts as symptoms in the
process of knowledge.
M. C. Richards

Our ability to commit to a creative life is also related to how much faith we have in our projects and in the creative process. Without faith, the necessary hard work and commitment can turn into drudgery. And the temptation of immediate gratification in other activities will drive us from our creations. If we have faith in the usefulness and rightness of our work, we will derive satisfaction from the process itself.

Fear is an unconscious choice based on wrong beliefs. You
can choose differently. You can learn there is nothing to
fear. Fear arises from lack of love, or lack of acceptance of
perfect love.
Willis Harmon, Ph.D. and
Howard Rheingold

Faith is trusting that the path you are on is the correct one. Faith engenders sacrifice. It allows you to surrender to the needs of the project and forgo your immediate needs for the sake of its accomplishment. The road to completing big projects is fraught with obstacles and frustrations. Without faith, you will quit before you turn the corner to success.

Faith is also the result of choosing projects that fulfill your deepest needs. When you answer a calling to engage your energy in a worthwhile project, faith is easier to find. You will have more tolerance for the frustrations and disappointments along the way. So, choose your projects well and keep the faith.

EXERCISES

★ 1. Have you made a covenant or bargain that you have forgotten about? Review your agreements with yourself and powerful beings. Do you want to renegotiate these agreements? Perhaps you want to clarify them or bring them up to date.

★ 2. Make an agreement with yourself or a higher power. Agree to give of your time and energy (perhaps a journey or charitable work) if you are given a helping hand in accomplishing one of your goals.

★ 3. Look at your resentments. Practice letting go of past bitterness. Forgive and move on.

★ 4. Make a public commitment to your project. Notice how it changes your energy level. Notice also that it may increase your fears and anxieties. Use an affirmation based on faith to alleviate these. For example, say: "I have faith that I am making the right choices and that the universe will help me reach my goals."

★ 5. Make it a point to spend some time by yourself. Solitude is essential in getting in touch with your inner voice. Listen to the silence within.

★ 6. Meditate on your blessings. Learn to see your glass as half full rather than half empty. Count your blessings. Be grateful for all the good things you have in your life.

★ 7. How much time and energy are you devoting to your various projects? Those are the measure of your commitment to your projects.

★ 8. What are your expectations for your various projects? Are your commitments (time and energy) commensurate with your expectations? If not, how can you increase your commitments?

Chapter 14

THE CREATIVE LIFE

'Come to the edge,' he said. They said: 'We are afraid.' 'Come to the edge', he said. They came. He pushed them . . . And they flew.

Guillarme Apollinaire

We have come to the end of our journey. From our early explorations of the nature of reality and the source of creativity, we have gone on to describe numerous tools and strategies for stimulating creativity. Along the way we examined myths and misconceptions concerning the creative process and debunked the myth that there is one creative personality type. We looked at stages in the creative process and ways to overcome creative blocks. To round things out, we explored the importance of environment in nurturing creative energies.

Summaries are often helpful in condensing a large quantity of information, but I think a summary would not do justice to some of the details presented in this book. Instead I will highlight some of the information we have covered. These are the essential truths about creativity and the creative process.

1. We are all creative all the time. We express our creativity in everyday activities such as dressing, dating, eating, cooking, selling and playing. Creativity may manifest in ideas, personal relationships, the production of an event (such as a

wedding, seminar, or conference) or in physical activity such as athletics or dance. In sum, labeling and organizing "reality" is a creative act.

2. Originality can be taught and, like many other things, it usually gets better with age. Originality comes from constant modification over a long period of time. It is the result of constantly finding problems and arriving at unusual solutions.

3. An average IQ is all that is needed for most creativity. And being creative does not necessarily mean being neurotic. In fact, some of the healthiest people are highly creative. There is no creative personality type. Each personality creates according to its own style. Being an expert or genius in one domain does not make you an expert or genius in another.

4. Creativity usually requires hard work. A project takes us through eight stages, beginning with receiving a call to do something. A challenge. As we proceed in our journey, we must assess our resources, do some research and then take action. Our adventure will require struggles and strategies. At times it will appear that nothing is happening and we are at an impasse. Most likely, incubation is taking place and our breakthrough is near. In allowing things to happen, we set the stage for catching lightning in a bottle. Polishing and refining are in the seventh stage, and celebration comes in the eighth stage. The end of one project means the beginning of the next. We may also experience a letdown at the end of a project. I call it postpartum depression. Don't worry, it will pass.

5. Your enjoyment must come from the work itself; otherwise, you won't have the energy needed to complete your projects. Although external rewards may be appreciated and serve to validate our efforts, the most powerful source of reinforcement for our behavior is the intrinsic value of our work. Act from your deepest values—from your passion center.

6. Hypnosis and affirmations are powerful tools to enhance creativity. Visualization unlocks the unlimited resources of your imagination. Among other things, it helps you get in touch with your psychic allies, overcome blocks, create a traveling laboratory, and recapture the energy of past creative moments. Your creative muscles can also be pumped up by doing lists and sketches, outlining, changing levels and perspectives, or dividing and subdividing a problem. You can use attribute listing and combine opposites to create new solutions. Change languages and experience a whole new universe of perceptions. These include the languages of dance, music and drawing. In addition, use humor to jolt yourself out of your usual perceptions and jog new ideas out of your funny bone. Program yourself to dream creatively.

7. In order to remain creative, you must learn to handle criticism. Don't overreact. Make allies out of your critics. Use the techniques in this book to build yourself up when you run out of gas. You have a right to be respected. Don't let your critics abuse you.

8. If you cherish your flashes of insight, they will eventually lead to lightning bolts of illumination. Be on the lookout for "aha," "wow," "that's it" and "I've got it" experiences.

9. Faith is necessary to keep you going through the many failures and rejections that are a normal part of the creative journey. Don't waste energy in search of revenge. Learn to forgive and let go. Most of all, learn to forgive yourself.

10. Live the creative life. Use creativity for good. Share your uniqueness and give back to your community. Creativity may be a gift from the gods, but just as important, it is a gift from you to humanity.

Throughout this book we have seen that creativity involves risk-taking, commitment, sacrifice and hard work. The bigger the project, the more energy and time is required to bring it to fruition.

Thomas Edison was right: creativity is 1 percent inspiration and 99 percent perspiration. You may avoid committing such amounts of time and energy to big projects, but you will also lose the satisfaction of accomplishing big things. The inspirational Kahlil Gibran poem, "On Love" *(The Prophet),* tells us that, if we shy away from the demands of love, we will cry, but we will not cry out all of our tears. In the same way, if we let fear restrict the life force to love unconditionally, then we will laugh, but never let out all of our laughter. Creativity is love. It comes from the same place. And the words of Kahlil Gibran apply equally well.

Although I didn't talk directly about child-rearing practices, advice in this arena can certainly be extrapolated from what I have said throughout the book. Thus, we should teach our children to be flexible and question authority. Certainly, challenging them with problems to solve would stimulate their creative imaginations. We should reward curiosity and imaginative play. Allowing children to have a say in rule-making, and negotiating with them in determining rewards and punishment for behavior, will instill positive self-esteem and encourage creativity. Give children room to grow and make creativity fun. Make them feel special and unique.

The best teacher, of course, is a good example. Lead a creative life. Always look for places to express the creativity skills and attitudes described in this book. Keep on developing new techniques and applying them in your relationships, at work and in your hobbies. Creativity is a way of going through life with the attitude that you are in control and that you have choices. You can change yourself and the world around you.

I trust that you have now learned that creativity is much more than applying this technique or learning that craft. Rather, creativity is the attitude we bring to reality. The Spanish phrase *Cada cabeza es un mundo* ("every head is a world") sums it up. Each of us is a value-maker and each of us has a unique reality to share with others.

Creativity is the key to making your dreams come true. I've discovered that all of the psychology self-help books are about creativity in one way or another. They all encourage the reader to be open and flexible and to take risks. Almost all these books are about giving permission to ourselves to be free of guilt and to allow ourselves to dream the impossible. These are some of the very things that I have been teaching about creativity. In essence, these authors are applying the principles of creativity to attaining good sex or achieving financial success. At the root of what these authors advocate are the creativity principles discussed in this book. Now you have some very specific, practical and powerful tools to help you reach your most cherished dreams.

Where do we go from here? The future is full of possibilities, and we are on the verge of a new era on planet Earth. The computer promises to truly transform the world into a global village. The Internet is in its infancy, but its potential power to link us into a true human family is awesome.

Look around you. The opportunities to express your uniqueness are everywhere. Use your creativity to improve your family, your neighborhood, your nation. Invite others to realize their creative potential. Encourage them to use their imaginations and try new ways of doing things. We need a continuous flow of fresh ideas and perspectives to guide us through the complex problems the world faces today.

What motivates us to create? For one, we create in order to express our unique visions and perceptions. We want to partake of the gifts bestowed by the gods. We want validation and a chance to be special or perhaps even great. But let us not forget that we also create to communicate and to form a bond with our fellow human beings. We create to contribute to the group and to give back some of the treasures we have received. Our creation is a gift, an offering.

Creativity can be explored and investigated, but it will never be fully known. I have given you many tools to develop and improve your creativity, but this is just the beginning of your exploration. Even though we can learn to improve our creativity, there will always be so much more to learn.

Creativity is the Self searching for itself and, in the process, remaking itself. Its full identity will never be known, for it is a mystery that never ends. It thrives on suffering and flourishes on joy. It is the universe revealing its never-ending possibilities. Its ideal is to live in the eternal Now.

Good luck, and keep on creating.

APPENDIX I
RESOURCES

Book Publishing

Publishers Marketing Association, 2401 Pacific Coast Hwy., Ste. 102, Hermosa Beach, CA 90254, (310) 372-2732, PMAonline@aol.com. Especially helpful for self-publishers.

Business

National Association for the Self-Employed, (800) 232-6273.

National Association of Women Business Owners, (301) 608-2590.

Small Business Administration, (800) 827-5722.
Good for loans and/or advice about setting up and running your business.

Computer Software

DecideRight, Avantos Performance Systems, (800) 282-6867.

Inspiration, Ceres Software, Portland, OR, (503) 245-9011.
See discount coupon offer at the end of this book.

MindLink Problem Solver, MindLink Software Corp., (800) 253-1844.
See discount coupon offer at the end of this book.

Educational

Adult Education Association of the USA, 1225 19th St. NW, Washington, D.C. 20036.

Association for the Study of Dreams, P.O. Box 1600, Vienna, VA 22183, (703) 242-0062.

National Home Study Council, 1601 18th St. NW, Washington, DC 20009.

The Learning Annex, 11850 Wilshire Blvd. #100, Los Angeles, CA 90025. Excellent classes on a variety of topics.

Film

American Federation of Television and Radio Artists (AFTRA), 260 Madison Ave., New York, NY 10016.

American Guild of Variety Artists (AGVA), 4741 Laurel Canyon Road, North Hollywood, CA 91607, and 184 Fifth Ave., New York, NY 10017.

Financial

Fidelity Investments, (800) 544-8666. No brokerage fees.

Schwab Financial Services, P.O. Box 52013, Phoenix, AZ 85072-9215. No brokerage fees.

Interior Design

American Institute of Interior Designers, 730 Fifth Ave., New York, NY 10019

Inventors

Inventors Workshop International Education Foundation, 7332 Mason Avenue, Canoga Park, CA 91305-2822, (818) 340-4268. Ask about their annual convention

Legal

California Lawyers for the Arts, Fort Mason Center, Building C, Room 255, San Francisco, CA 94123, (415) 775-7200. Low introductory rates for artists.

Volunteer Lawyers for the Arts, 36 West 44th St., New York, NY 10036. Low introductory rates for artists.

Music

Firefly, http://www.agents-Inc.com "for people who love music and want to make new discoveries."

National Academy of Songwriters, (213) 463-7178. Workshops, pamphlets and newsletter.

Songwriter's Collaboration Network, (310) 828-9378, http://www.earthlink.net/~songmd/.

Songwriters Guild of America, 6430 Sunset Blvd., Ste 1002, Los Angeles, CA 90028. Workshops, pamphlets and newsletter.

Songwriters Guild of America, 276 Fifth Ave., Suite 306, New York NY 10001, SGANews@aol.com

Worldwide Music, The Internet Worldwide Web site for independent record labels, P.O. Box 1582, Davis, CA 95617-1582, WEB SITE: http://wwmusic.com/~music/, e-mail: music@wwmusic.com.

Real Estate

Apartment Association of Greater Los Angeles, 621 So. Westmoreland Ave., Los Angeles, CA 90005-3902, (213) 384-4131. Services for landlords. Informative magazine and various legal forms and credit check services available.

National Association of Real Estate Boards, 155 E. Superior St., Chicago, IL 60605.

Writers

The Author's Guild, 234 West 44th St., New York, NY 10036.

Writers Guild of America, East, 555 West 57th St., #1230, New York, NY 10019.

Writers Guild of America, West, 8955 Beverly Blvd., Los Angeles, CA 90048.

Miscellaneous

Grantsearch, Leigh F. Wright, 2674 Johnson Pl., Baldwin, NY 11510, (516) 223-4117.

Institute of Noetic Sciences, 475 Gate Five Road, Suite 300, Sausalito, CA 94965, (415) 331-5650.

National Endowment for the Arts, 1100 Pennsylvania Ave. NW, Washington, DC 20506.

National Association of Artists' Organizations, 1007 D St., Washington, DC 20002.

The Gray Panthers, 3635 Chestnut St., Philadelphia, PA 19104, (215) 382-3300.

World Future Society, 4916 St. Elmo Ave., Bethesda, MD 20014, (301) 656-8274.

Workshops

George Gamez

Creative Solutions Workshops based on methods presented in this book are available. Other materials on creativity, such as a newsletter, are also available. See order form at end of book or contact me at (213) 655-8777.

APPENDIX 2
BIBLIOGRAPHY

Amabile, Teresa. *The Social Psychology of Creativity*. New York: Springer-Verlag, 1983.

Amabile, Teresa. *Growing Up Creative*. New York: Crown Publishers, 1989.

Arieti, Silvano. *Creativity: The Magic Synthesis*. New York: Basic Books, 1976.

Blunt, Anthony. Picasso's "Guernica". New York: Oxford University Press, 1969.

Cameron, Julia. *The Artist's Way*. New York: Jeremy Tarcher/Perigee, 1992.

Capra, Fritjof. *The Tao of Physics*. New York: Bantam Books, 1976.

Chung-yuan. *Creativity and Taoism*. New York: Harper and Row, 1970.

Daix, Pierre. *Picasso: Life and Art*. New York: Harper Collins Books, 1993.

Edwards, Betty. *Drawing on the Artist Within*. New York: Simon and Schuster, 1987.

Einstein, A. et al. *The Principle of Relativity*. New York: Dover Books, 1923.

Fobes, Richard. *The Creative Problem Solver's Toolbox*. Corvallis, OR: Solutions Through Innovation, 1993.

Fritz, Robert. *Creating*. New York: Ballantine Books, 1991.

Grinder, John, and Richard Bandler. *Trance-formations*. Moab,UT: Real People Press, 1981.

Gardner, Howard. *Creating Minds*. New York: Basic Books, 1993.

Garfield, Patricia. *Creative Dreaming*. New York: Ballantine Books, 1979.

Ghiselin, Brewster (editor). *The Creative Process*. New York: Mentor Books, 1952.

Harman, Willis, Ph.D., and Howard Rheingold. *Higher Creativity*. Los Angeles: Jeremy Tarcher, 1984.

Huxley, Aldous. "Vulgarity in Literature," Music at Night. 1931.

Jones, Michael. *Creating an Imaginative Life*. Berkeley, CA: Conari Press, 1995.

Kasha, Al, & Joel Hirschhorn. *If They Ask You, You Can Write a Song*. New York: Cornerstone Library, 1989.

Klauser, Henriette Anne. *Writing on Both Sides of the Brain*. New York: Harper Collins, 1987.

Koenenn, Connie. "The New Neighborhoods: Creating Connections Out of Chaos." Los Angeles Times, May 12, 1994.

Kremer, John. *1001 Ways To Market Your Books*. Fairfax IA: Open Horizons, 1993.

LeCron M., and Jean Bordeaux. Hypnotism Today. No. Hollywood, CA: Wilshire Books, 1978.

Levinson, Jay Conrad. *Guerrilla Marketing*. New York: Houghton Mifflin Company, 1993.

Maisel, Eric. *A Life in the Arts*. New York: Jeremy Tarcher/Putnam, 1993.

Maisel, Eric. *Fearless Creating*. New York: Jeremy Tarcher/Putnam, 1995.

May, Rollo. *The Courage to Create*. New York: Bantam Books, 1978.

Miller, William. *The Creative Edge*. New York: Addison-Wesley Publishing Co., Inc., 1988.

Nachmanovitch, Stephen. *Free Play*. New York: Jeremy Tarcher/Putnam, 1990.

Olson, Robert. *The Art of Creative Thinking*. New York: Barnes and Noble Books, 1980.

Panter, Barry (editor). *Creativity & Madness*. Burbank, CA: AIMED Press, 1995.

Patrick, C. *What is Creative Thinking?* New York: Philosophical Library, 1955.

Powers, Melvin. *How to Get Rich in Mail Order*. No. Hollywood, CA: Wilshire Book Company, 1988.

Ray, Michael, and Rochelle Myers. *Creativity in Business.* New York: Doubleday, 1989.

Samuels, Mike M.D. and Nancy Samuels. *Seeing with the Mind's Eye.* New York: Random House, 1992.

Schlipp, P. *Albert Einstein: Philosopher-Scientist.* Library of Living Philosophers.

Simonton, Dean Keith. *Greatness.* New York: Guilford Press, 1994.

Sloane, Paul & Des MacHale. *Challenging Lateral Thinking Puzzles.* New York: Sterling Publishing Co., Inc., 1993.

Sloane, Paul & Des MacHale. *Great Lateral Thinking Puzzles.* New York: Sterling Publishing Co., Inc., 1994.

Storr, Anthony. *The Dynamics of Creation.* New York: Ballantine Books, 1993.

Swami Beyondananda. *Driving Your Own Karma.* Rochester, VT: Destiny Books, 1989.

Thompson, Charles. *What a Great Idea.* New York: Harper Perennial Publishers, 1992.

Von Oech, Roger. *A Whack on the Side of the Head.* New York: Warner Books, Inc., 1983.

Von Oech, Roger. *A Kick in the Seat of the Pants.* New York: Harper & Row, 1986.

Wujec, Tom. *Five Star Mind.* New York: Doubleday, 1995.

Weisberg, Robert. *Creativity: Beyond the Myth of Genius.* New York: W. H. Freeman and Company, 1993.

Wells, Valerie. *The Joy of Visualization.* San Francisco: Chronicle Books, 1990.

INDEX

ABOUT THE AUTHOR

George Gamez, Ph.D. is a licensed clinical psychologist and a professional musician. He is President of Psychological Center and the Executive Director of Creative Solutions.

He is a member of the National Academy of Songwriters, the American Songwriters Guild, and the National Academy of Recording Arts and Sciences as well as the California Psychological Association, the California Society of Industrial Medicine and Surgery and the American Psychological Association.

As a psychologist he has taught at the University of California Santa Cruz, and at several California State Universities. He currently conducts creativity workshops for graphic artists, screenwriters, actors, songwriters, entrepreneurs, and lawyers.

As a musician, his work has been recorded numerous times. He co-wrote the song "Bridges of Love" which was recorded by Jose Feliciano, among others, and has written songs for children's educational TV. His own most recent CD, *Lightning Strikes Again*, includes "Nuevo Flamenco" guitar instrumentals and songs which were inspired by his work on creativity.

In 1991 he ventured into the world of event production and promotion. The "Latin Music Expo" was a highly successful conference attended by the most creative and productive minds of the latin music industry.

George Gamez is currently the host of his own cable TV show "The George Gamez Show" where he talks about creativity, performs his music and interviews guests.

AN INVITATION

I would love to hear from you. Feel free to write to me regarding your experiences as a creator. Let me know if and how this book has helped you. Anecdotes and examples are most welcome. If you have any comments or questions about the contents of this book, please share them.

Write to me at the following address:
George Gamez, Ph. D.
C/O Peak Publications
P.O. Box 451067
Los Angeles, CA 90045

My Internet address is create@gramercy.ios.com.

Order Form

Fax order: (213) 655-7509

Telephone orders: (213) 655-8777 OR (800) 600-8207

Postal orders: Peak Publications, P.O. Box 451067, Los Angeles, CA 90045.

Internet e-mail: create@gramercy.ios.com

Please send the following:

☐ *Creativity How to Catch Lightning in a Bottle* $14.95

☐ Free newsletter "Creative Solutions"

☐ *Lightning Strikes Again* CD $14.99

☐ *Lightning Strikes Again* Cassette $8.99

☐ Free brochure

☐ Self hypnosis cassette tape of script "Deep Relaxation" in Chapter 7 $10.95

☐ Free speaking engagement calendar

Company name (if applicable): _____

Name: _____

Address: _____

City: _____ State: _____ Zip: _____

Telephone: _____

Sales tax:

Please add 8.25% for books, cassette tapes or CDs sent to California addresses.

Shipping:

Book, CD or Cassette: $2.00 for each item and 75 cents for each additional item.
Air mail: $3.50 for first item and 75 cents for each additional item.

Payment:

☐ cheque

☐ credit card: ☐ VISA, ☐ MasterCard, ☐ Optima, ☐ Amex, ☐ Discover

Card number: _____

Name on card: _____ Exp. date: ____ /_____